About the Author

Maritza Durán is a researcher who investigates the impacts of global migration. She makes her home in the Pacific Northwest of the United States with her husband, children, and grandchildren. In this magnificent place, she continues the lively, loving, and resilient story of her family clan.

From the Dictators' Shadows: A Family's Journey

Maritza Durán

From the Dictators' Shadows: A Family's Journey

Vanguard Press

VANGUARD PAPERBACK

© Copyright 2025

The right of Maritza Durán to be identified as author of
this work has been asserted by her in accordance with the
Copyright, Designs and Patents Act 1988.

All Rights Reserved

No reproduction, copy or transmission of this publication
may be made without written permission.
No paragraph of this publication may be reproduced,
copied or transmitted save with the written permission of the publisher, or in
accordance with the provisions
of the Copyright Act 1956 (as amended).

Any person who commits any unauthorised act in relation to this publication
may be liable to criminal prosecution and civil claims for damages.

A CIP catalogue record for this title is available from the British Library.

ISBN 978-1-83794-459-0

*Vanguard Press is an imprint of
Pegasus Elliot Mackenzie Publishers Ltd.*
www.pegasuspublishers.com

First Published in 2025

Vanguard Press
Sheraton House Castle Park
Cambridge England

Printed & Bound in Great Britain

Dedication

Dedicated to the loved ones who came before me, and those who traveled with me.
"There is freedom waiting for you,
On the breezes of the sky,
And you ask, 'What if I fall?'
Oh, but my darling,
What if you fly?"

Erin Hanson (2014)

Acknowledgments

My family's courage has guided my life and the writing of this story. My goal has been to be a family storyteller for my children, grandchildren, and all who will come after. This story is for you: Chris, Beth, Haley, Cooper, Ray, and Rose. As you make your way across the world, it is the resilience of kin that must enlighten and inspire you, even in this age of virtual ghosts. My life is blessed with a life partner and friends who have loved and supported me. Beloved Greg, you walked every step of this journey with me. Thank you, even for the times I balked at your feedback. Nancy, you have been my wisdom reader, going deep between the lines and showing me what I was afraid to say. You are a wonderful friend. My other writing colleagues, Susan, and David, you have been a safe place, so very generous in your presence, direction, and support. Tracy, you gave me such good advice. It started with you, Dee, one visit at a time. Your writing gusto and style led the way for me. Kirsten, you were the first editor to set eyes on my manuscript, I so appreciate your being a part of this process with me. Chris, my photography consultant, what would I do without your eye? And then there is

Cooper, my researcher, who traveled across time and place making sure my compass was set straight. Thank you for being such a champ. I am grateful to the Pegasus staff for their unique skills in shaping this project towards its completion. My special thanks are to you, Lesley, for your gracious and steady hand. You have shepherded me through a wonderful experience during a unique juncture in my life.

Name Key

Maria Stelladora   *Maritza; Patti's daughter; Narrator of Part 3*

Rosina Dorada   *Rose, Rosie; oldest of the Burgos Beltrán sisters; Narrator of Part 1*

Petra   *Patti; youngest of the Burgos Beltrán sisters Narrator of Part 2*

Nina Maria   *Nina; one of the Burgos Beltrán sisters*

Estrella Martina Burgos de Beltrán   *Mamá*

General Bernardo Beltrán   *Papá; the General*

Manuel   *Milo; oldest of the Burgos Beltrán brothers*

Dionysus   *Dio; one of the Burgos Beltrán brothers*

Victor   *Baby Victor; youngest of the Burgos Beltrán brothers*

Enrique Pérez Gomez   *Hero and founding father of the Puerto Rey Republic; ancestor of the Burgos Beltráns*

Raul Galante   *President and Dictator of Puerto Rey; El Pulpo; Big Galante; Big G*

Israel   *Servant and protector of General Bernardo Beltrán and his family*

Lola   *Close friend of the Burgos Beltrán family and godmother to several of their children*

Tita   *Housekeeper and cook for the Burgos Beltrán family*

Tia Teresa   *The General's sister and children's caretaker*

Fernanda   *Milo's wife*

Rubiroso Murillo   *Rubi; mayor of Las Piedras who accompanies the Census takers*

Zoraya and Nino   *Cousins of the Burgos Beltrán sisters who assisted in their resettlement in New York*

Manuel Goya   *Rose's first husband in an arranged marriage*

Bobby and José   *Sons of Zoraya and Nino*

Millie Brecher   *Rose's best friend and business partner in New York*

Jorge Gavilán   *Rose's second husband*

Gabriel Acosta   *Patti's deceased husband and Maritza's father*

Julia   *Victor's wife*

Margie and Mary Murillo *Maritza's neighbor friends at the Dollhouse*

Victor, Jr., Harry, Ronny, Anita *Victor's children*

Prologue
The Dream

My name is Maria Stelladora, but my family calls me Maritza. I was born in New York City and grew in the loving arms of my mother Petra and the lively spirits of my namesakes: my mother's sisters, Rosina Dorada and Nina Maria, and their mother Estrella. Their fiery love was meant to be a fortress against the crushing death of my father only weeks after my birth. Sent to live in the tropical sunshine during summer, I was schooled there in *clases de señorita* (young lady lessons) away from New York City's roller-skating, ringolevio and much later, Greenwich Village dance clubs.

When I was about eight years old, I began to have a dream. A family of six, dressed in summer white, is standing on the veranda of some important building in the capital city of Puerto Rey. They are all squinting as they face the bright afternoon sun. The mother shields her eyes against the glare and the bullet aimed at her head. The biggest boy screams, as his father is hit in the temple at close range. Then another bullet pierces the boy's own abdomen. The two younger children are blinded by the wounded bodies that fall against them. And the girl's, lace-edged socks are splattered with blood.

Where did this dream come from? Sometimes it was a story that also came to my mind in the daytime when I played in New York's Riverside Park. It came when my mother, Petra, moved closer to me as she watched a man watching children on the slide. It came when she and I walked home alone from a night at the movies, or when she answered a ringing telephone that was a wrong number. Ever vigilant of the space between us, Mom often looked like the mother squinting on the veranda.

At home, I was never quite comfortable falling asleep alone in my room, but I was eventually lulled by my family's quiet talk in the kitchen. It must have been then, piece by piece, when those murmurs formed the story, I thought was a dream. The people in white were my family in the Caribbean island nation of Puerto Rey, and in 1955 when I was almost eight, government agents opened fire on them. My uncle, Victor Burgos Beltrán, once his family's little prince, was killed instantly. His wife and my four adored cousins would be wounded for the rest of their lives.

Living in the United States, I was a lucky one: the child of one of the three Burgos Beltrán sisters, Rosina, Petra and Nina, who migrated to safety in North America in the 1930s. Their brothers, Victor, Dionysus, and Manuel, stayed behind on the island, fighting the tenure of one of the most sadistic rulers in Latin American history: Raúl Galante. They fought the war against *el pulpo*—the octopus, as he was known. These boys, together with other boy cousins, would eventually be murdered, made to disappear, or *maltratados*—the delicate Caribbean word used in social company for torture. Their lives formed a long wake of sadness that erupted around Puerto Rey's Caribbean Sea, then floated far north into the Atlantic as the family migrated to new lives—from the edge of the Florida Keys to New York Harbor to the eastern coast of the French Canadians.

Today, we Puerto Rey descendants in the United States know who we are. We live the story on the veranda in every fiber of our beings. The story permeates the ugly parts of the world we choose to see, as well as the beautiful people we have chosen to love. As we matured, we learned that our formation was more complex than we ever imagined. We come from a time when the Burgos Beltrán clan was part of an audacious group of people who helped shape a democracy out of Puerto Rey's soil. With tenacity, conviction, and courage, our kin fired the hearts of all of us who came later. Using our own signatures, many of us became fighters against injustice and powerlessness. Others embraced our family fire in a different way— vowing lives of peace, spirit, and the reverberating power of love.

This is the story of our Puerto Rey family. My aunt Rosina Dorada – Rose – wove together the pieces of our family's early years over many hours of being with me. She was my other mother, Petra's older sister, and the matriarch who knew every secret. Rose begins our family story in Part I. My mother Petra, who saw the world through gentle hope, tells us about the beginning years of our family after migrating to the United States, in Part II. She kept her eyes firmly fixed on her own American dream.

Finally, I'll come back to you, in Part III. This is the hardest part for me to understand—my place along the long road traveled by my people and my family. How does my life fit into theirs? Maybe it does, but maybe not. I'm getting closer to the completion of my own time in the world, and this period of recounting has illuminated me. But it has been so much easier to tell you about everyone else!

All of the voices who speak in this story have done so through the filter of my own experience and memory. I've tried to recount things as best as I can, checking with historical documents, genealogy charts, and many, many aunties along the way. As for the inevitable story gaps and spaces, I have sewn them together with the deeply colored threads of our Puerto Reyan culture.

PART I
Rose

Rose
1
Our Beginnings
Puerto Rey, 1897

In 1897, I was born to Estrella Martina Burgos and General Bernardo Beltrán, in the lush countryside of Puerto Rey. My name is Rosina Dorada, Rose or Rosie if you like. I am the first teller of our tale and the oldest of my parents' six children. Our father, a zealous patriot, named each of us after a flame of hope for our country. What a ridiculous man! My name means "golden rose." It stands for our country's natural beauty, strong stem, and ability to protest when not treated with dignity. I was told many times the rose can pierce, despite its perfumed charm. What this all had to do with me, I have no idea. Just call me Rose.

Mamá and *Papá* gave birth to two more little girls and three boys. The girls were Petra Cristina, the rock of our faith, and Nina Maria, a colonial patriot. The two oldest boys were Manuel, after a political scholar, and Dionysus, the Roman god of merrymakers—because despite their hardships, our people have a twinkle in their eye and love a good joke. And finally, there was the last child, Victor, a name chosen deliberately by *Mamá.* By the time this baby came along, she was sick and tired of naming her children for the hopes of this sweaty, backward, illiterate and corrupt country: so, she named the baby after Queen Victoria. No tinge of anything patriotic for this one. Hah!

Mamá was Estrella Martina Burgos, the genteel and educated daughter of Catalonian Spaniards. Despite the Burgos' residence on the Caribbean island of Puerto Rey for three generations, these artists and businessmen had preserved their continental manner and very important blue eyes. These were coveted qualities for our *Papá*, General Bernardo Beltrán, an ambitious military man who smoothed his crusty edges with the cultured strains borrowed from his young wife. The General, as he was known, was descended from the Gomez clan, a clever, educated and pistol-whipping line of the country's early founders. Our ancestor, Enrique Pérez Gomez, was not only one of the early fathers of our country but a physician who performed surgeries when he was not gunning down French colonial soldiers in the fight for a free Puerto Rey republic. Our ancestor Gomez was among our country's early *mestizos*, the magical blend of ethnic threads that gave birth to the Puerto Reyan people we are today; a mixture of races created by our indigenous groups, Spaniards, and Africans.

Our story has taken almost two hundred years to live, and almost one hundred of my own life to tell. I've recounted the tale over many spaces of time to Maria Stelladora, who we call Maritza. She has lovingly written down my words. Maritza is my niece, who should have been my daughter. Through some scramble in the cosmic shuffle, she was born to my little sister, Petra. But no matter, this girl and I knew who we were to each other the moment her soul flew into her body.

You already know about the catastrophic event in 1955 that killed my youngest brother, Victor. A member of a secret cell that distributed information about President Raúl Galante's horrible crimes, he was assassinated for treason by the dictator President's military police. He was the baby named after the genteel Queen Victoria—the baby whose life our poor *Mamá* hoped would not be touched by political turmoil. How ironic life is. The massacred Victor is now a national hero of the Galante dictatorship's resistance, with a monument in his honor placed in a city plaza.

I'll begin by telling you about my childhood, introducing you to my family and taking you into my early womanhood.

Rose
2
Life and Home in the Capital City
Catalina, Puerto Rey, early 1900s

My family's home in the capital city of Catalina was always a hubbub of activity. The house was on *Calle Flores*, which was close to the harbor. Encircled with lacy verandas and blooming flowers, the Burgos Beltrán residence looked like a two-tier birthday cake. It was painted salmon pink – all the rage in turn-of-the-century Caribbean capitals. The house's rosy glow cast a spell on our entire household. My rambunctious sisters and brothers jumped from veranda rails onto adjacent palm trees; housemaids-in-love called after street vendors; and someone was either tacking up a bucking horse or riding one in the small back pasture that was home to the General's two cavalry mounts and *Mamá's* pretty, white pony.

The buzzing center of this hive was our father's study. The large wood-paneled room took up one whole side of the house. We were forbidden to enter, except when accompanied by the General himself. Ha! This was a joke because at least one of us children tried to break in every day. The study's walls were lined with tall library cases and polished cabinets inlaid with designs on the doors. Brass fittings held the cabinet doors together. Our brother Dionysus, we called him Dio, used to say they looked like soldiers with shiny buckles, standing at attention.

When the General was in good humor and not perspiring too much, he would choose one of us to come into his inner sanctum. If he only knew the backroom drama over who would be the next child visitor to his study? I always felt *Papá's* invitations to me were special ones. I was the oldest, after all. In spite of my sharp antennae, I never knew beforehand what our visits would be about. He might show me a map of the island's many winding rivers, reverently pulled from the tall map cabinet. Or he might let me touch the silver handgun in the glass case, used by our ancestor, Enrique Pérez Gomez to fight the French colonials. A few times he showed me the oldest and yellowest map of his collection: the first diagram of Catalina, the new colonial city, and one of the earliest in the Americas. This old map showed secret routes to the river's docks. Working in the President's administration, our father had access to many special documents that both provided details for his job and furnished information for his own soon-to-come political purposes.

I always knew when my special time with *Papá* was coming to an end. There was a signal. He walked over to the French doors and courteously led me outside toward the line of palms at the side of the house. Planted specially to form a long walkway of breezy relief from the heat, this was the very walk the General took with his important gentlemen visitors. And now he was escorting me through the grove. *Papá* had this curious habit: he saved the most important part of his visit for the walk outside. He'd turn to me with a serious face and say something like, "I show you these things so you'll understand how hard we are trying to make our small, now free country, a good place to live, where everybody has a real house and doesn't have to be afraid when a *guardia* (police officer) knocks on their door."

Then his face got sad, and I thought maybe he was going to cry. As a little girl, I felt so important when he talked to me like this. I was proud of him. I would remember everything he told me so that later when people said things about him, I tried not to listen.

Rose
3
The Coup That Crushed Our World
Catalina, Puerto Rey, 1911

For most of 1910 through 1911, our house was in an uproar. Dispatch soldiers ran in and out with messages at all hours of the day. *Papá* met with men dressed in fancy suits, late into the night. We knew when they had been there because his study reeked from cigar smoke in the morning. It was a jumbled mess of coffee cups and papers all over the floor. The family and servants knew something was going on, and that the General was wrapped inside the storm. But what was it?

I wondered if *Mamá,* his trusty confidante, knew. She was almost at the end of her forty-day confinement after the birth of her last baby, Victor. She was strong and healthy over these last years. There was no sign of her consumption coming back. I knew because as her oldest daughter, I watched her like a hawk. I *needed* for her to be okay. What Mamá knew of the events that were occurring will always be a mystery to me. But she expressed as much surprise as the rest of the household when on the Tuesday morning of Easter week in 1911, *Papá* disappeared before dusk with a small group of men on horses. So said Israel, our helper and nightwatchman, who never slept.

While everyone in the stunned household was congregated in the front hall that morning, Dio made a dash for *Papá's* study. He considered himself its unofficial security guard since he was the only one who could pick the door lock. The room was a shock. The silver pistol was gone from its glass case. Finding the tall cabinets open, Dio saw that the diagrams of the capitol buildings were gone too. As far as he could see, gone were the floor plans to the Senate House, the Presidential Palace, and the *Capitolio* (capitol building).

I made a run for the stables behind the house. *Papá's* horse, Capitán, was missing from his stall and so was his military tack. Cappy's breastplate with our country's silver medallion wasn't hanging from its hook. And the heavy endurance saddle was not there either. I calmed myself down for a minute, to think.

"It's Holy Week, there wouldn't be any big parades going on today. I knew it! Capitán had been tacked up for fighting. And now he and *Papá* were gone!"

We children ate our breakfast with *Mamá,* in silence. We were off from school for the religious holidays and so hung around the kitchen hoping to hear some information about what was going on. *Mamá* received some men visitors and talked with them. Coming out of the parlor after they left, she had a very serious expression on her face and immediately gathered the household. I was a little annoyed she didn't pull me aside, as the oldest, to talk to me first about the serious thing that was happening. She ordered all the doors and shutters to be locked and no child was to leave the house, not even to the backyard. Some trouble was going on in the capitol building, maybe fighting, and *guardias* were all over the streets keeping order. That was all she said, then she went into her bedroom to nurse the baby.

I knew something was very wrong. After an hour, restless and dying of curiosity, I tiptoed into her bedroom to see if I could help with anything. *Mamá* was dozing, I thought, and holding the baby close. As I turned to leave, she quietly said, "We have trouble, Rosa. It's your father. He and his men are involved in confronting the President. We all know what a despot that *jefe* (president; the boss) is, but trying to get rid of him by force? That's too much, even for your father's *cojones* (balls). How is this going to turn out? I have no idea. Your father listens to no one when it comes to his beloved *patria*—he's *un loco* (a crazy man) sometimes. Just help me keep everybody calm, and don't tell the children your father is in this. And don't talk to any of the servants about it. You hear me? We won't hear from your father for a while—whether things turn in his favor or out of his favor. Here, take baby Victor and walk him around the inside garden while I take a rest."

"Si, *Mamá,*" I answered, as I took the little baby bundle and left *Mamá's* room. I found the baby pram and went round and round our inner courtyard, lost in my own worried thoughts. Was this what all the men at the closed meetings in the study were about? Was *Papá* doing a good or a bad thing? None of my parents' friends liked the President. I knew that. I heard them talk. And I knew the servants were all scared of the government police. But my big question was: exactly how much did my mother know about what my father was planning? As close as I was to her, the line stopped at her relationship with *Papá*. I had no idea whether she really loved him, agreed with what he decided or dared to stand up to him... The inside of their marriage was a mystery to me. That day, *Mamá* told me about *Papá's* fighting the current government, as well as *Papá's* brief jailing some months before. He and three or four colleagues were charged with collecting and hiding guns in the countryside. Hmm, so that's why he was gone for a whole month. At that moment, though, my job was to help *Mamá* as much as I could, keeping the children happy, and ignoring everyone's questions about where our father was.

Days went by, then weeks. Military law was declared in our city, so no one was allowed out of their homes at night. Only two hours of shopping time were permitted during the day, and schools didn't reopen after the Easter holiday week. Soldiers and police were out looking for the "enemies of the Republic," "perpetrators of the chaos," and "cowards who will be shot." The tension in our house was terrible. Every one of our servants was interrogated by the police. Israel was grabbed in the front yard and taken to the precinct for questioning. I didn't know then what "interrogation" could mean. The women servants were harshly questioned in our kitchen.

We busied ourselves and tried to forget our worries as best we could. The cook baked flan after flan. *Mamá* let the little ones splash in the courtyard fountain in their underwear. Sewing by hand because she still didn't know how to work the Singer sewing machine *Papá* had gotten her for her birthday, *Mamá* managed to make herself an entire summer dress. Then one day, when we thought we would go crazy for the hundredth time, a soldier came to the door with *"un mensaje muy importante para la Sra. Burgos de Beltrán"* (a very important message for Mrs. Burgos de Beltrán). *Mamá* ran to her room, stayed there for several hours and then came out to tell us the plan.

Rose
4
Estancia Bella
La Loma, Puerto Rey, 1911

It was settled. After four months of nothing from *Papá*, he finally sent word he would be coming to the house in a disguise to pick up *Mamá* and the baby. They were to accompany *Papá* way into *el monte* (the forest) to the West. Dressed as poor farm people, the little family of three would travel on the road, supposedly looking for work near the other side of the island. No one from the capital city with *un solo chele* (a single cent to his name) would look for work there. It was very poor there, a place where previous slaves lived, and where those who managed some work lived from hand to mouth.

In a cart pulled by an old donkey, the well-known General, participant of the failed coup, was now a miserable *pater de familia*, hoping to escape capture by the militia. Can you believe it? The general-peasant had the *nerve* to drag along his just-delivered wife, and infant child. What a crazy man! It was a ridiculous plan. I begged *Mamá* not to go.

"Please, please don't go with him. Something terrible is going to happen to you. *Papá* is putting you and the baby

in terrible danger. He's using you, *Mamá,* he's using you."
I told you before, that there was a part of my mother I never understood. Did she obey her husband because she loved him *and* feared him? To this day, I don't know. What I do know is, from that day, I began to close my heart to my father.

Of course, I was the one to stay behind in the city, watching over the other children. *¿Yo?* (Me) I was terrified. What if my parents disappeared for good?

"We'll send for you. Don't worry, don't worry," said *Mamá.* "*Papá* will hide for a good long time until things settle down and they stop looking for him. I'm only going as a disguise for him, to situate him, to get him to the hiding place. I'll leave him there and meet you children in a few days at *Estancia Bella*, our cacao farm in La Loma. It's only for a few days, *hija,* (daughter). You'll stay here in the city with Israel, then I'll let him know when it's time to bring you all to meet me at the farm."

So *Mamá,* with baby Victor nursing quietly at her bosom, set off with Papá early the next morning just before sunrise. We never actually saw *Papá* for ourselves. He stayed in hiding until the last moment of jumping onto the buggy bench and clicking quietly to the donkey: "*Vamos, que Dios nos guie.*" (Let's go, may God be our guide.) Taking the dusty road out of the capital city, they passed others who looked just like them; but these farmers were coming *into* the city with carts of *yuca* and *plátanos* (plantains) to sell in the central market. At least, at this point in the journey, they blended well with the others. But if you looked closely, you might notice the farmers' eyes hooded with sleep, while *Papá's* eyes squinted with fear. He nervously clicked the old donkey forward toward the open road to the West. *Mamá* sat quietly beside him. Crying? Raging? Spitting? Hating her husband? I'm not sure. All I know is that to prepare her for this deadly charade, we cut her lovely nails down to the quick, dressed her in a torn skirt and bodice, and padded her with plenty of undergarments because she was still bleeding from the birth. "*Dios mío protéjala.*" (My God, protect her.)

I do not know, and no one I've ever asked knows, what transpired in the forty-seven days our parents were gone. Somehow a dwelling, a hiding place in a high cave had been arranged for them by a very loyal soldier friend of *Papá's*. But we know the man never arrived at the meeting place. They say the militia got him, killed him and made him disappear because they knew he was loyal to the General. We'll never know...

What we knew was that *Mamá* and *Papá* were not discovered. That's for sure because we would have heard. While that was a relief, our household in the city was nevertheless a den of weepy children asking constantly when our mother would return.

"Where is our baby?"

"What if they never send for us?"

I calmed them as best I could, but I was terrified inside. Then, on the forty-sixth day, Israel finally got word that we were to meet *Mamá* at our farm in the outskirts of La Loma. We would leave at dusk the next morning and get there by the midday meal. Everything was being prepared for our stay at our *Estancia*, by the workers who always lived there. Everyone was expecting us, and – best of all – *Mamá* would be there waiting!

While the three-hour wagon trip to the farm was long and bumpy as usual, we were all so excited about being together again. We couldn't wait to see baby Victor, as we called him in English, even though we hardly knew him. We believed him to be our tiny baby doll. As for *Papá*? Well, our feelings there were confused because he had done such a big thing that the militia was looking for him. We were afraid of that. Maybe he should stay away for a long time. Besides, we were used to his being away on soldier jobs for months.

Estancia Bella's house stood alone on fifty *hectares* of mostly cacao groves and some cattle pasture. Those ugly plants that grow pods like giant beetles finally give you chocolate. Carved out of the rainforest by our uncle Pablo, *Papá's* brother, our place was nestled in a green valley where the earth was black and moist and nourished by underground aquifers. All around us was the deep tropical jungle to the West that went on and on until the end of the world. This was the direction in which *Mamá* and *Papá* had gone. The workers believed great walking timbers lived there. These monsters entangled lost people in their vines. If you went in there, you might never come out.

Rolling toward the farmhouse entrance, we spotted our flamboyants first, fiery red trees planted by *Mamá* to show the liveliness and strength of our family. We listened for the birds nested in their branches and the chatter of people who were usually everywhere on the farm: field workers, animal tenders, aunties who took care of us. But moving forward, we noticed everyone was gone. The machines in the fields were quiet, and no one was outside the house. Empty were the rockers on the big front porch, usually occupied by the affectionate helpers who always awaited our arrival. This was strange because they knew we were coming. In fact, no one was on the *Estancia* except for our wagon of children and Israel, who had driven us in from the capital.

"Wahoo!" The kids jumped out and were running everywhere.

"Look at the mango trees. Let's climb them and get some!"

"I'm going to check my pony," said Dio.

Patti and Nina, three and four, giggled as they took off their sandals and walked tiptoe on the green tickly grass.

"*Niños, adentro ahora mismo.*" (Children, inside, right away.), I called, frightened by the silence.

We explored the house, the bedrooms and the backyard; but no one was there. We stood and stared at each other.

"Where's *Mamá*? I want *Mamá*," Nina started to screech.

I called for Israel. He was somewhere outside. Suddenly the black bell by the big front gate entrance to the *Estancia* started to clang and clang. That scared me because no one who knew our place rang that bell; they always knew to come in by the side road. I was afraid to go. I waited, waited, then I heard Israel down by the gate entrance say in his deep, I-have-a-gun, country voice: "*¿Quien es?*" (Who is it?)

Dio and Manuel (who we called Milo), were impatient little boys as always, running down to see what was happening. Israel yelled, "*No ábran.*" (Don't open.) But the boys opened anyway. To this day, I'll never forget the sound of those boys' screams. To their horror, they found their mother thrown on the ground, bloodied, barely conscious and bound by lengths of dirty fabric that held the baby to her back. Was the child alive? Baby Victor was silent, but his enormous eyes were open—deep mirrors of knowing.

"*Mamá*, oh *Mamá*." She stirred, began to cough and cough and spill bright blood from her mouth. Her bodice was wet and dark, and stained with her sickness. I don't remember what we did next or how we passed the following hours of the afternoon. Somehow, we managed to wash *Mamá* and get her into bed with the baby finally nursing at her breast. Evening came. The baby's eyes seemed to never blink: they just stared at all of us huddled around, close together.

I remember it was a windy evening because I heard the little bumps of the cacao pods swinging against each other in the breeze. I mark the evening time because it was at dusk, in the darkening, that *Mamá* died. Estrella, our thirty-year-old mother of six children was gone.

We stood like a carousel of little mourners around her big mahogany bed. We, the older ones held the younger ones as Mamá turned her face to the wall for the final time. The baby was still at her breast—Victor, the little prince, splayed across her body. *Mamá* tried to hold him until the end, but when she turned, she let go of her grip and the boy rolled to her side. It was then I knew.

As *Mamá's* room darkened and her face faded in the shadows, I panicked. The air was hot and thick with the sweet smell of lilies I just noticed on her bedstand. Who put them there? Did someone know she was going to die today? My mind was exploding. I wanted to be sick. Just then, Nina whispered softly to me, "When is *Mamá* going to move?"

I pretended not to hear.

We stood still by the bedside for a long time. It was baby Victor who first stirred, rousing us with a wail.

"It's getting dark," said Milo.

"What if no grownups come to light the lamps? Israel said the workers all ran away this morning."

"It's hot in here," murmured Dio. "Someone needs to change the baby's diaper."

Petra who was almost three, clung to my blouse and said in her baby voice, "It stinks like poo."

I told her to hush. But how can you be cross with a toddler whose mother was dead?

Estrella Martina Burgos de Beltrán, *Mamá*

Oddly returning to their playful selves, the little boys began to fidget with *Mamá's* pretty things spread all over her bureau. Even in the country house, Estrella insisted on keeping her beautiful things around her: the shiny crystal lamps that were lit all day, the tortoise brushes that untangled her long hair, her leather Bible, Dio's paper hearts, and the tiny enamel box for the ruby ring that was *Papá's* wedding present.

Our father had indulged his young wife like no other. While most of the house was modestly furnished, Estrella's bedroom was a sight to behold, especially on this night. The room had been decorated all around with huge French mirrors. These glittered against the blue-papered walls. Now, a multitude of bewildered children bobbed in their reflection. Estrella's progeny.

I thought if I didn't speak or move, my tears would not spill over, nor my stomach turn. But finally coming around, I did like the little ones, and began to fret over what had to be done. There was dinner and bed, and making the children comfortable for the night. She would want this. So, I finally signaled my new charges by marching out of *Mamá's* room. First, gently lowering Petra from my arms, I then took baby Victor to my bosom. I felt his damp baby cheek resting on mine. I wondered if he could feel the pounding in my head.

We crept down the dark hallway as we left our mother's room. The floors were stone cold and echoed from the fall of our steps in the unfurnished hall. The plan of the house was a circle that surrounded an inner courtyard. The march took us from the dark hallway through the courtyard garden and finally into the kitchen and storerooms at the back of the house. The children squealed as they hopped through the courtyard garden. They hated crossing it at night. That was when the palmettos cast shadow-tentacles on the grass with their spindly leaves. *"¡Arañas!"* they screamed. *"¡Tarantulas!"* Milo and Dio stabbed the *spiders* with sticks they had somehow been holding all afternoon. They were just little boys. They would need sticks for the rest of their lives—the only way to beat down the vision of their fallen mother at the front gate.

We ran through the spooky courtyard, to be met by a dark and gloomy kitchen, barely lit by embers from the morning fire.

"Boys, start lighting the lamps. Niños, sit around the table while I cook." What do I do if they start to cry? With all the courage of my fourteen years, I charged the stove and focused on what I could feed my brood who had not eaten since I didn't know when. The lamps finally illuminated the kitchen, bringing a tiny dose of life into our sorrowful group.

Rose
5
Under the Mistresses
La Loma, Puerto Rey, Colegio Metodista, 1911

After a sad dinner of burned rice and black beans – no meat or fish – it was all I could find, I gathered the children into the girls' bedroom. I don't know where my bossiness came from, but I snapped at the boys to bring in every mattress they could find and make the room one big bed. We would all be here until I figured out what to do, who to call… Oh God! Where was Israel, where were the workers? It was now the black dead of night. Only the screaming *grillos* (crickets) and snapping *cacaos* kept us company. I tried not to think of our *Mamá* lying cold in her bed. For the children, there were no baths, no washing and no pajamas tonight. We just fell like six whimpering weights, onto the bedding—all together and never so alone. Sleep came instantly.

In the middle of the night, there was terrible pounding on the front door. The voices of women called, "*Niños, niños, ¿están bien? Venimos para ayudarlos. Ábran la puerta.*"

"Who is that? Should we open? It's women. They say they come to help us."

The little ones start to cry from the noise. Dio and Milo say that they still have their sticks and will back me up at the door—such funny boys. I go to the door with the baby in my arms and open it only a little, when the bodies of two very big white women wearing cinched long dresses and straw hats, bustle into the front hall saying, "We know about you children, we know what's happened here."

The one with a big bosom and shoulders who calls herself Miss Laura, suddenly grabs the baby from me and cradles him in her tremendous arms. I panic for an instant, but the big lady's kind blue eyes and the sight of Israel right behind her at the door tell me she's good. The other lady is very tall and thin and carries an umbrella cane she uses to gently get me and the boys out of her way.

"My name is Mrs. Wimble," she says. "I am an American nurse. Take me to the rest of the children." She sees my confusion and whispers gently in my ear, "We are teachers from town, we have a school for children. We'll take care of you there. Don't be afraid. You're Rosa?"

"Yes," I say.

She caresses my face which makes me cry and says, "Show me where your dear mother is lying."

I barely have a recollection of the rest of that night. All I remember is that the ladies took charge and packed our clothes into two big sacks, which Israel carried out and placed at the back of their horse-drawn wagon. One black horse and one chestnut stood patiently awaiting orders. Then our Israel carried each of us up into the back of the wagon, treating us so gently. Covering us with blankets, he told us to sleep and that we would be okay now.

I remember feeling mad at these bossy mistresses: where were they taking us; how dare they decide things for us, and how could they be the ones holding our baby at the front, while they clicked the horses forward?

"What are you doing? What are you doing?" I screamed. "I'm the oldest, Rose."

But we went faster and faster out of the dark night of our farm, up a hill, through some of the mysterious blue forests, and finally out into an open road that headed toward the center of the town of La Loma. Before I could think, cry, or fight any more, I must have gone numb and fallen asleep together with the others.

When morning came, we awoke to find ourselves in a strange place. It was a school maybe or a hospital? Many beds were in the room and I rushed to make sure we were all there: Petra, Nina, Milo, Dio and me—but where was the baby?

I screamed out, "Misses, Misses, help, where is our baby? Where is our Victor?"

The big lady and the tall one came running into the room telling me to shush. "Baby is all right, sleeping. You are all together now, here at our school, *El Colegio Metodista,* the Methodist School. Children study and board here, and you'll be students here for a while."

I started to cry as the rush of yesterday's events and the death of *Mamá* came crashing into my mind like a train. I started to cry again when the big one, Miss Laura, cradled my shoulders with one of her enormous arms and led me gently out of the dormitory into a small room that looked like her office. The room was painted sunny yellow with many pictures of children hanging on the walls. Books were stacked high on every table, and above her enormous mahogany desk, kind of like *Papá's,* was a large cross.

After sitting me down and giving me her hankie to wipe my tears, she brought me a hot cup of *café con leche* (coffee with milk) with some buttered crackers—the same kind of breakfast I had at home. A part of me wanted to like her, she always seemed to know what I needed the moment I needed it. But I hated her and that other skinny one. Their Spanish was terrible, it sounded like they had beans in their mouths. They were American. But they had us.

I started screaming again. "How can this be? How can this be? What happened here? Where is everybody? Dead. Dead! *Mamá is* dead and *Papá* is a fugitive. I don't know if he's a good person or a bad person…"

I quieted down and drank my *café*.

After taking the last bite of my breakfast cracker, Miss Laura looked straight at me with her tiny, strange, blue-cloud eyes, and said in her accent, "Listen to me now, you are not orphans or our charges. You are full boarding students at our School just like the forty-seven others we have. Your General father provided money for schooling and care in case he had to be away. Let me say right away," she emphasized. "We know he's in hiding, we know what he's done, and to us he is a patriot."

My God, that was a relief! At that moment I thought he was a patriot too!

"You and the rest of the children will go into your grades and learn with us until it's time for you to go home." She continued, "And, don't worry about baby Victor, he's in our care."

"What?" I said. "He's in *my* care, not yours. He's my baby brother."

"*Calma, calma*, Rosa," Miss Laura answered. "You can be with him any time you're not in class, whenever you want."

To tell you the truth, I think I scared that big white lady. Good!

Miss Laura's expression turned sad when she began, "Now we have to make arrangements for your mother. We're in touch with Israel and your godmother, Lola. They tell me there is a little cemetery on your farm, on a hill between the fields and the forest."

Tearfully I said, "Yes, it's a holy place, people are buried there because it's where their spirits can fly quickly up into heaven. *Mamá*… would like that…, I think."

"And so it will be," said Miss Laura. "Your godmother, Lola, will come tomorrow to be with you children. She'll bring your proper clothes for the funeral and stay, pray and be with you until it's time to go to the burial at three o'clock."

"I'll dress the children, I'll dress them," I said a little too loudly.

"Okay, okay," quietly whispered the blue-eyed lady.

Lola arrived early the next morning with Israel, who had gone to fetch her and many of our belongings from our home in the capital. Lola was godmother to most of us and our mother's very close friend. Her heart must have been breaking, but her mission on this day was to give us some much-needed love and comfort. Also, at this time, I had no idea of what energy and care Israel had given to our family. He rounded up the workers to prepare the burial, and he even paid off the local La Loma police to not disrupt the funeral by searching for *Papá* at the farm. From what I learned later, Israel withstood more than one beating when questioned about the General's whereabouts. They threatened his life. At this moment though, he was all smiles when he entered our dormitory with Lola, carrying suitcases and bags filled with our books, clothes, toys, and my girl things. Tiny four feet ten inches Lola was practically knocked over from the strength of our hugs and kisses. We were so happy to see some piece of our real lives, and people who we belonged to.

At exactly two fifteen p.m. the next day, we marched out of the school like silent little soldiers and climbed up into the mistresses' now familiar horse-drawn wagon. We girls were all dressed the same in our white Sunday dresses, tied at the back with pastel ribbons. I remember thinking how odd it was for me, an almost young lady of fourteen, to be dressed the same way as Petra and Nina, who at ages three and four, still toddled on their feet.

Something enormous happened to me the night before. My heart and maybe my body grew a hundred times, as the force to protect *Mamá's* children enveloped my entire soul. I guess we all grew that night. So somber were my little soldiers, that Dio and Milo, looking handsome in their dark pants and white *guayaberas* (an open-necked linen shirt worn by men and boys in Latin America), did not even skip, wiggle or talk to the carriage horses. And the diminutive girls walked in a single file with the others, insisting on not being carried. After all, it was the solemn day of their *Mamá's* burial.

No one spoke on the carriage ride. As always, the approach to the farm took our breath away as our farmhouse, the barn buildings and vast cacao fields looked like a miniature world curled inside a green bowl of rainforest all around. The carriages entered the front gates held open by two of our workers. Sweetly, solemnly, they removed their hats and bowed their heads to us as we passed, as did all those lining the path that led to the burial hill beyond the fields. When the wagons stopped, we silently jumped off and did what *Mamá* always instructed us to do when we first arrived at the farm. We took off our sandals to walk along the warm black soil of the planted fields.

"Feel that earth," she always said. "Bury your feet into it as you walk. It is your country loving you."

When we got to the burial place, many people were gathered around the hole in the ground. I don't remember too much, just some pictures that will never leave my mind. When the rough wood box with *Mamá* inside was lowered into the hole, we began to throw shovelfuls of dirt as a way of saying our final goodbyes, but the children started losing control. Milo and Dio threw fistfuls of dirt, then shoved mounds of it over the lowered coffin with their bare feet, screaming and crying. The little girls started too, until it was impossible. There was no way to stop them. Miss Laura and Mrs. Wimble finally scooped up the little ones and took them away, down the hill. Two of the younger workers held the boys and took them away too. The next thing I remember is standing alone by *Mamá's* grave with cold hands and the feeling that my life was changed forever.

"How do I take care of your children, *Mamá*? Will the General ever come back? Am I in charge?" I started to say the only prayer I know by heart: *Padre Nuestro*, Our Father.

I don't remember anything else about that day.

Rose
6
Alone
La Loma, Puerto Rey, Colegio Metodista, 1911–1915

There we were at the *Colegio Metodista*, for God knows how long. I won't lie, we were well taken care of. In the arrangement my parents made, we had more than safety, clean beds, meals and an education. We had heart. The schoolmistresses did their very best to comfort us and tolerate our antics. They let us cry, be a nuisance, and even be a little naughty—within reason, of course. The little girls, Petra and Nina, spent their days in the nursery room with the few other younger children who also boarded at the school. Matrons in pretty, yellow uniforms took care of this chattering little crew, with Mrs. Wimble at the head. Mrs. Wimble was such an odd lady. She walked along the school corridors as if there was a broomstick stuck in her very tall back. Her bony head and tight grey bun framed a face that hardly smiled except... yes, except when she was with her babies. It was as if you saw a person melt. Mrs. Wimble dropped her long body onto the floor, lowered the tone of her voice, and played with those toddlers as if she were one herself.

Our Petra asked her one day, "*Missy Wimby*, why is your nose so big?"

The teacher laughed and laughed, taking Petra into her long arms and squeezing her. After one of these moments, she pulled herself up, smoothed her bun and said something like, "Play is healthy for children. I know about this because I am a nurse from the United States of America." This was her *mantra*, one we would later imitate when we were in silly moods.

Petra and Nina seemed to be settling well enough during their days, but it was the nighttime when the terror and tumult of the recent months showed themselves. We six children slept in our own dorm, separate from the others at the school—because I insisted. They were mine at night, to comfort me and I, them. Baby Victor's crib was next to my bed, and the little girls were on my other side. The girls wet their beds almost every night—nerves, you know. The only way it wouldn't happen is if I took them in my bed and let them fall asleep cuddled against me. Those poor little things... Finally, I just asked the matrons to put diapers on them. I had to get some sleep.

Then, there was baby Victor. He was happy and playful in the nursery with his little sisters but soon was full of coughing and wheezing that made him into a delicate baby. By the time he was nine months old, the olive skin of his smiling face was stained with purple circles under his eyes. His big brothers made him laugh and laugh with silly faces and animal noises, but it wasn't long before the baby's hearty laughter turned into coughing and more coughing. Sometimes the coughing turned into choking at night, at which point I called for Mrs. Wimble. She came immediately to place the baby in a small steamy room where she ran hot water. After holding and calming Victor down, she usually put him to sleep in her own room—a relief to me, which I would never admit. When I thanked her the next day, taking the baby from her, she said cheerily, "I know what to do for him. I am a certified nurse from the United States of America." I had to laugh.

Milo, the oldest boy, was fine. He just underwent an entire personality change at the school, that's all! From being his brother Dio's partner in silly antics, he became a total fan of two big B's: books and baseball. The boy turned inward, serious and focused on devouring as many books as he could. History of any kind appealed to him – Roman gladiators, American cowboys, and Vikings of the North. And he didn't leave our Puerto Reyan history aside, reading everything he could lay his hands on about Enrique Pérez Gomez, a founding father of our country and our ancestor, according to *Papá*. The other big B was baseball. That boy's long arms were powerful: it looked like his left one was driven by a motor. Using his precious Chicago White Sox glove and a softball (gifts from the American mistresses), he pitched perfect shots, time after time against the schoolyard wall. I frankly think the boy was simply enjoying himself, out of the critical gaze of his father. *Papá* was always hard on him. For Milo, I guessed the reactions to *Mamá's* loss would come later.

My little brother Dio worried me. A character of his own. There were pranks from him every day and secret gatherings with other naughty boys. He went into the headmistresses' very private bedrooms and put baby spiders into their toothbrush cups. He turned all the crosses in the school – and there were many – upside down. In the classroom, he put forbidden bubblegum into the braids of the little girl who sat in front of him. One evening, as we sat in the dining room for dinner, he finally tested the patience of the mistresses, who suspended him from class, for a week.

Like the dorm room, we had our own table in the dining room. It opened onto a courtyard of tropical flowers and many hanging birdcages. Yellow canaries and parrots of every color chirped and sang for our meals. On this day, I turned to pass the bread to the boys and Dio was gone. Gone from the table, but I could hear his distinct high-pitched laugh. He was chirping, loudly, like a bird, and laughing in between. But where was he? By this time all the children in the room were making a *rebulú* (a ruckus) and looking for the source of the sound.

Finally one yelled, *"Mira, es Dio caramado en las ventanas, vestido como una cotorra."* (Look, it's Dio climbed on top of the windows, dressed like a parrot.) Everyone pointed up, and there he was. Wearing a crazy cape costume and flapping his arms like wings, he hung from the high window cornice. Pretending to be a giant parrot, he threatened to fly down into the dining room. *Ay, yay, yay*. What were we going to do with this boy? His behavior was getting more out of control, going from funny to disturbing. And who was the little group of boys he spent time with? Were they encouraging him? This time, I gladly left the situation to the mistresses.

And me. Yes, me. I didn't know how to think about myself; I just worried about the children. How long were we going to stay here? Would *Papá* ever come back to get us? Had he disappeared? Even I could see how extreme these burdens were for a fourteen-year-old girl. But I had no room to be sad or outraged. I had my special moments in the mornings when I woke ahead of the children. I spent this time talking to *Mamá*. What should I do today? How do I take care of the baby? Should I let Mrs. Wimble be more in charge of him? How do I find out where *Papá* is? My questions, my fears and my sense of aloneness went on and on. But I had a trick. If I kept my mind still and didn't cry, I think she would talk to me. She told me what to do. I just had to make my mind quiet enough to listen.

Months, then almost four years went by as we tried to make the best of things living at the *Colegio*. Two things saved my soul during that time. One was that the mistresses made me the special head girl of the students. That meant I helped keep the children in line: I talked to them when they needed me. And sometimes I helped in class when the mistresses were absent. Some of the other children at the school were lonely little ones like our own, whose parents were away working, or who had suffered the tragedy of a mother dying, like ours.

"Rosa," Miss Laura said. "What a capable girl you are!" She praised my easiness with numbers and gave me a little job, for money. I worked in the office and kept track of how much the school spent on books, building repairs and endless supplies. Deep down inside, I knew I liked how I was, but hearing it from someone I came to respect, was different. Yes, I said respect! The truth was that I let go of my rebellion toward Miss Laura (most of the time), and finally surrendered myself to her kindness, and even love. Who else did I have to love me then?

The second thing that kept me alive and hopeful was our Lola's visits. My godmother was there, every Sunday, like the stroke of the big clock in the school's front hall. What a love she was, bringing homemade things for a big meal. We always started with her fish *croquetas* (croquettes), which the boys grabbed in fistfuls.

"*¿Niños, niños, que hacen?*" (Kids, kids, what are you doing?)

I remember the exact Sunday, and what we had for lunch, the day Lola gave us the biggest news in the world. We had *ropa vieja:* shredded beef in tomatoes and peppers, affectionately called old clothes because of the messy way it looks. There was *Moros con Cristianos:* Moors with Christians, bronzed yellow rice with red beans mixed in. As always, Milo, our history professor, told us the story of this dish based on the Moors' occupation of Spain in the 1100s. The dish showed the new and different colors of the people in Spain at that time. Just like every Sunday, the mistresses came over to the shady back porch where we ate our Sunday lunch and offered a fresh green salad to go with the meal. We all giggled when we saw them coming with their big wooden bowl.

In loud whispers, the boys said, "*¡Es que quieren comer comida Latina!*" (It's that they want to eat real Latin food!) They were right. On Lola's invitation, Mrs. Wimble and Miss Laura protested only the tiniest little bit, to join us for lunch. Those polite ladies sat themselves down and ate like horses!

Waiting for ice cream after our big meal on that day, Lola said that she wanted to make a special announcement. The mistresses smiled at each other, as if they knew the secret.

"Niños, en exactamente dos meses, vuelven a su casa." (Children, in exactly two months you're going home.)

"*¿Y Papá, y Papá?*" we asked.

"Your father will be coming home, too."

I sat there frozen in shock. The children yelled and screamed and ran around the table. Even baby Victor, now almost four and being crazy like the others, giggled, "*Si, Si, Si,*" not having a clue what was going on. Was this real? Lola looked at me in the middle of the children's happiness, signaling that we would talk about the plan after lunch.

After our meal, it was so hot that even the boys joined the little ones napping for their siesta. Lola and I took our usual walk around the schoolyard, settling on a bench under a flaming flamboyant full of blossoms. It was a tree like the ones *Mamá* had planted in front of our country home: a good sign, a symbol of strength and beauty. Lola assured me *Papá* was now a free man, no more running. He was made to understand by Lola and others how much we children had endured, with no parents in our lives for such a long time. Lola said that *Papá* had arranged for our arrival, and we would be well taken care of even though our own precious *Mamá* was gone.

So, fifty days after that Sunday, we children were in the familiar rear of our own wagon from home, driven by Israel. Only the feverish baby, Victor, stayed behind with the mistresses until his health improved. We were finally going home. It was the end of an era for us.

Rose
7
Home at Last
Catalina, Puerto Rey, 1915–1918

I was told by Lola that *Papá* had made thoughtful arrangements for our care, upon the return home. That plan for our lives was planted right on the front porch as we pulled up to our city house in Catalina. Standing erect with her arms on her hips was, oh no, *Tía* Teresa, Aunt Teresa, our father's older maiden sister. And, sitting, fanning herself on a porch rocker was our *Abuelita, Papá's* three-hundred-year-old mother. Oh, no! In an instant, we saw it all: our aunt, the mother-general of the house—like we needed another general! And our grandmother, who was a little cuckoo sometimes, but at least had the biggest, softest bosom in the world for soothing tears. What was going to happen now?

Tía's orders started immediately. "*Niños,* kiss your *Abuelita,* (little grandmother) and go to your rooms. Wash, change your dusty clothes and come to the parlor in thirty minutes."

"Wait a minute, wait a minute," I said to myself. I could feel my jaw tighten as I almost became just another one of the children taking *Tía* Teresa's orders. I screamed inside myself: "I'm the biggest girl, the oldest and the one with the brains and the heart. I take care of *Mamá*'s children, not *Tía*." So, I decided to show *Tía* who I was from the very start.

We gathered in the parlor as ordered, and I deliberately took a chair and placed it right next to *Tía*. I was about as tall as she was, and with the dress and little heels I had changed into, I looked very grownup. Just to make sure, I sat with my straightest back and my chin slightly lifted just like Mrs. Wimble's. I wanted it to look like there were two women in charge. In her snappy voice, *Tía* told us that she was running the house with *Papá*. Obedience was holy; and she would not stand for any loud noise, commotion, or mess from us. She turned red as she spoke and little bubbles of spit sat at the corners of her mouth. The boys started to giggle, then the little girls, then me. It was so embarrassing as *Tía* looked around, confused, with the *coraje* (temper) taken right out of her. I almost felt sorry for her.

Tía Teresa had always tried to be a good sister to *Papá* and a dutiful daughter to their parents. Now she was trying to take care of our family mess: six orphaned nieces and nephews she barely knew, and a brother who disappeared on political raids. You see, Teresa was the appointed child in her family. By that, I mean the tradition in our Latin countries for an unmarried daughter, or sometimes a son, to take care of the old parents and any other family burdens. Teresa was unmarried—an old maid, as they called these ladies. She knew love once, as a girl, but the boy died, and she never gave her heart to anyone else. Now at forty-seven, she was bitter, lonely and without charm. Worry filled her now, as well as a heavy sense of duty which she believed came from God.

But, for the moment I'm telling you about, I confess that I used all the strength I had, to take advantage of my poor aunt's weakness. In my most grownup tone, I said, "*Niños, niños, respeto, respeto.*" (Children, children, respect, respect.) Then I say, "Both *Tía* Teresa and I, your big sister, will take care of you. You'll do your same chores. Dio and Milo, you will collect the laundry every day and take it to the tubs, to be washed. Petra and Nina, you clear the plates after dinner and take them into the kitchen."

"*Tía* Teresa," I say, "With all due respect, I have watched over these children for the last almost four, very hard years. I will continue helping them with school and solving their everyday problems."

Tía just stared at me without a word. When I nodded, the little rascals marched out of the parlor. I followed them in my wobbly heels and best posture. The moment was over. Stunned, as she saw us all filing past her, *Tía* was dribbling at the sides of her mouth, and said in a shaky voice, "Your f-f-father arrives in three days."

I tell you, we spent those three days deliciously exploring every corner of our own rooms, the house, the yard and garden, and the back stable that housed our three city horses. We pulled out every toy and game and gadget that was part of our lives when *Mamá* was alive. Some of those things were broken and needed to be thrown away. In general, the house was clean and organized, kept up by the servants during the long, long time we were gone. I'm sure that *Tía* and *Abuelita* made the house sparkle for everyone's arrival.

The only mess was in the General's study from when soldiers and police tore everything open, looking for information on the failed plot to overthrow the now previous government. Even after all this time, no one in the household dared touch this room. *Papá* would organize everything when he got back.

It's so strange the way things happen in our Latin countries. You keep silence, hide your opinions, and even go into hiding if you've offended the government. But then, in the snap of a popular election or the pop of a bullet into a president's head, everything changes. It's a new day in your capital! Can you believe *Papá* was now considered a minor hero by some people, for trying to get rid of the last president? I'm not totally sure but what I can tell you is that when *Papá* came home to us to reorganize his life, he accepted every praise and every compliment he could to secure a good position in the new administration. And when he didn't get enough of that, he initiated political projects in his own way. After all, he was a patriot of our little republic of Puerto Rey and a fighter for his people, first and forever.

Life at home became a regular routine with two very big exceptions: the monumental hole left by *Mamá's* death, and the tension of my new job as "co-captain" of the household with *Tía* Teresa. I didn't let my guard down for a minute. The children were my job and my love. I did my best to offer as many kisses as I could to the little ones who slowly, and so sadly, began to forget their cries of, "*¿Donde está Mamá?*" (Where is *Mamá*?) So hard for me to witness this. Would I forget her as well?

I was working hard at finishing my *Bachiller* (high school diploma) and learning as much as I could about sewing and tailoring from Lola. Making ladies' dresses was a practical thing to know. As for *Papá,* he kept himself very busy working for the new government. At least, thank goodness, he wasn't leaving us again and getting into dangerous things… yet.

Tía Teresa and I, though, were always on the wrong side of each other. We disagreed on disciplining the children, what they should eat, how they should behave, and how I should comport myself. I heard *Tía* talking to *Papá* about me at night after she thought I was in bed.

"You have to control her, Bernardo. She has no respect for me. You'll see, she's going to get away with something big someday!"

Mamá and *Tía* had never really gotten along, and I certainly wasn't going to get along with *Tía* either. The simple reason was that the beautiful Estrella took the sour Teresa's little brother away from her. And, adding salt to the wound, our mother, Estrella, was a cultured lady and far more educated in every way. When Teresa suggested that I got my uppity ways from my mother's people, *Papá* raised his voice and said, "How dare you ever suggest anything negative about my Estrella!" That was the cue for Teresa to leave *Papá's* study. Poor *Tía,* she did try her best. I know I was difficult and so were the other children.

I have to admit, though, that *Tía's* best accomplishment was running the daily activities of the household itself, in the most efficient way. This was her esteemed brother's castle, after all. I remember the first night *Papá* gathered his new political group of like-minded gentlemen in the small house next door, a house he had purchased for the purpose of establishing a political headquarters.

As was our way, those who ate at home relaxed in the shade of the back porch after dinner. *Papá* sat in his big mahogany rocker, smoking *Don Pedros*, and *Tía* Teresa with sleepy *Abuelita* sat in little rockers, clicking their fans. I was at our godmother Lola's for my evening sewing lessons. I could make patterns now. Milo was out playing baseball with his boys, and Dio was at the movies. It was only Nina and Petra at home that night, playing in the backyard. On this Tuesday evening, there was no sign of the day's heat retreating.

"No breeze from the palms tonight," declared *Tía* in her usual bossy tone. But in the garden beyond the trees, Nina and Petra saw something in the back garden that Israel had taught all of us: the leaves on some of the bushes were starting to curl. This was a sure sign that it would rain and cool things off. It was a thrill for them to know more than the know-it-all *Tía* did!

As the story goes about that night, at exactly seven thirty p.m., *Papá* shook off his after-dinner haze, stood up from his rocker, and in full voice, started barking orders at his household of women. "The Generalissimo" – as Nina called him – commanded: "As we have discussed, *niñas* (girls), coffee, cigars and ice water are what we will serve at the political meeting tonight. Thank God, the paint and new mahogany floors have dried in the new house next door. I have enough problems trying to unite these mavericks into a political party! I don't need sticky floors to put them in a bad mood!"

Papá's new group called themselves something like the "Popular Party," and someday they intended to present their own candidate for president. This individual, they said, had to be a solid man who represented the party's platform: to develop the country's interior, build schools and hospitals, cut roads into the capital city, and of course eliminate corruption. *Papá* went on and on about how the country needed to teach *all* of its rural people how to read, write and grow their businesses.

This was a special night, thought *Papá*. *Tía* Teresa would simply not do for serving at the gathering. Her dreary face and faded black mourning clothes could sour any man's disposition. Instead, the girls would have to serve – Petra and Nina, twelve and thirteen – still girl enough, with only the hint of buds that wouldn't be noticed by the roomful of men's eyes, thought *Papá*. They still wore girlish dresses tied at the back with bows. Nina would probably be dazed by the sea of strangers, but Petra could guide her.

Tía Teresa was not happy with this arrangement. Weighed by her virginal ill temper, *Tía* took the well-being and running of her brother-general's home very, very seriously. Now tonight, the safety of the girls was in her hands. Two innocents at a gathering of God knows what kind of men was simply not proper, she thought. A secret that we children had figured out a long time ago was that *Tía's* sternness was really the bitterness about her own life.

So *Tía* Teresa was in a real state on this night. "Get those cups washed, dry them. Are the silver trays polished? Petra and Nina, the water is ready for your baths. Don't get your hair wet. When it's time for you girls to serve the coffee, Hortencia and Tita will carry the trays across the yard from our back door to the meeting hall next door. Then they will hand them to you. Everyone has to work quickly so the coffee stays hot. If you drop them or get any coffee on the saucers, you know what you'll get. Nina, none of your dreamy business. Pay attention to whatever Petra does. Those trays will be heavy, but at least we're using the demitasses. When you serve a gentleman, you know not to look at his face – keep your eyes politely down and pay attention to the tray – he will help himself to his own "*tasita de café*" (demitasse of coffee)."

The night could not have been more successful! Our *Papá* actually inspired his group of mavericks. As it was described in the paper the next day, *Papá* and his colleagues spoke eloquently to an audience that was clearly like-minded about developing the economy of Puerto Rey by elevating and educating the common man. The donor commitments made that night to the forming of the new political party, gave *Papá* deep satisfaction. But he was equally tickled by the newspaper's photo, depicting his elegant presence at the assembly, accompanied by two beautiful little girls on each side, carrying silver trays of demitasses: *The General Bernardo Beltrán and his Two Daughters of the Republic.* This was a title that Nina and Petra were forced to endure for decades. The story of this hectic night never failed to make all of us laugh until we cried.

Rose
8
Unique Children – Patti and Baby Victor
Catalina, Puerto Rey, Early 1920s

Over the years of my own growing and trying to mother *Mamá's* children as best I could, I came to understand how little ones live with sadness in different ways. It makes some fierce and bossy, like me. Or fierce and silent like Milo. Some get lost in the dark places inside them. Dio had no one to tell him that his ways were not devilish. As for Nina, wheels seemed to be turning all the time in her mind; she would never tell you what she was thinking. I think there was something complicated going on inside her.

Let me tell you now about our sweet Petra. I called her my Patti. I gave her that name when she asked me one day what it would be like, to live in America. This surprised me because I'd never heard her to be curious about the United States.

"If you go there, they will call you Patti," I said to this very serious little girl. And she gave me one of her rare big smiles—a sign, I guess, that the idea of America was living quietly in her mind. Her formal name was Petra Cristina. It meant Rock of the Christian Faith. Can you believe parents would give a child such a name? But who knows, maybe she did carry the strength and courage of our country in her sweet and serious little self.

Patti never felt herself to be a pretty child. She complained that her cinnamon-colored face was too long—like a broomstick, and her nose was too flat, like *Papá's*. A flat nose in our family was code for a black person's nose. And in a country like Puerto Rey, where everyone hated their African roots, this was not a good thing. Patti didn't like these things about herself, wishing that she looked more like her *Mamá*, whose ivory skin and blue eyes were envied by everyone. This feeling went very deep in her, I think. I'm not a psychologist, but I always thought Patti believed that if your loving mother dies and leaves you forever when you're three years old, the least your *Mamá* could do was give you her resemblance. Instead, your *Mamá* leaves you looking like your father, who you barely speak to and who is kind of scary.

As she got older, Patti invented pretty ways of dressing: from matching hair ribbons to her flowery dresses, to making sure her white sandals were spotless. Was she trying to lighten the imprint of her loss? Or was she inspiring herself for a future? To me, she had the look of someone who was waiting for something, but I never knew what that was.

How did the loss of our mother impact this gentle child? Did she even remember the touch of Estrella's hand? At three, Patti stood around our mother's bed with the rest of us. She saw Estrella's face turn into the shadows of her room at dusk. She heard baby Victor cry as *Mamá* released her grip on him. She trudged along the dark hallway and sat in the lonely kitchen with the others waiting, as I fumbled to make dinner-without-a-mother. Did Patti remember any of this?

This child never made a fuss. She never cried; she never asked where her mother was; she did everything she was told to do—obedient and tidy, and clearly the tiny force behind Nina, her older sister by one year. Patti was *presente,* alert to everything around her, responsive to others, but rarely showed her own desire. Where were her feelings? Were they buried so deep inside her, that not even she could find them?

Patti came to life more when she started school—chatty and laughing at silly things like other children. But there were stretches of quietness. She was present without a word, but oddly vigilant whenever direct action was needed. This was the new and unusual part of her: quiet, quiet, then bang!

Late in the afternoon of a very hot day, I was sitting on one of our front porch rockers finishing some of *Papá's* bookkeeping. I was distracted by the flies landing on my sweet lemonade. Suddenly I heard a group of children across the street, sing-songing and teasing Patti and Nina who were quietly and steadily walking arm-in-arm in front of the group. My little sisters were neither looking at the stinkers behind them, nor running away. But as they came within view of our house, Patti swiftly turned around, kicked the main teaser in the shins and gave her a hard push that landed the girl in the arms of the other children. Without breaking their pace, my two sisters walked to the corner, crossed the street, and entered the safety of our house. What do you think of that?

The girl was a mystery. You didn't know Patti was heated up or excited about something until you found her in the act. She was missing for lunch one day when she was around eight years old. We looked all over the house and finally found her alone on the back porch, digging into a tub of sweet golden mangoes, with the biggest smile on her I'd ever seen. Her explanation? "I just love them." What a funny little thing! Not only did I love Patti, I respected her. I learned a phrase much later, after many years of living and working in New York: Keeping your counsel. That's exactly what this child did all her life. And to tell you the truth, I could have used some of that myself.

Then there was our brother, baby Victor, who slowly grew into Victor, the boy. He actually never returned home from the boarding school with the rest of us. Victor grew up away from us, in the hands of his two foster mothers, Miss Laura and Mrs. Wimble at the *Colegio Metodista*. He seemed to have no time for sadness. This boy, who lay as an infant in the arms of our dying mother, appeared to have grown untouched by the trauma of her tragic death. As far as we could see, he was a happy, healthy, sporty and very, very smart boy. In addition, we slowly discovered a depth of spiritual life in him that was sure to influence his life. Maybe we should have all stayed at the *Colegio* with the mistresses. The ladies marked Victor's progress in beautiful letters they wrote to us every few months:

Esteemed General Bernardo, Rosa and children,

We hope this letter finds you and the entire family in good health, by the grace of God. Thanks to the Almighty, we find ourselves well and progressing with our ministry and school. We now have one hundred and ten full-time students in our charge and have hired a new teacher from the U.S. for the primary grades. This now makes six on our faculty. God has blessed us, indeed!

We are happy to tell you that your boy, Victor, is thriving and growing taller by the week. He has not had a grippe or coughing illness since we began giving him the vitamins we received from a pediatrician friend in Milwaukee. These are now given to most American children. Victor is filling out and stands almost as tall as the boys from the upper grades. He continues to be a studious and well-behaved child, as you know, who has never given us a moment of concern or trouble. On the contrary, he fills our spirits and small home with light. He is a happy boy. We believe he is developing a gift for the Scripture, as he not only reads but memorizes passages from the Gospels. Where his pious spirit comes from, we do not know. Possibly from his deeply buried infant memories of his dear late mother, Estrella, reading the Bible out loud.

We are proud to say that Victor's sense of justice and what is right, are also very developed for such a young child. The other day he insisted we bring a confused man into our school, who was begging for food outside our front gate. Mrs. Wimble nursed the man for a few days until he was stronger, and your son Victor prayed with him every morning.

General, you know that we take the responsibility you have given us with Victor very seriously and believe the stability and care we offer Victor has made him a strong boy, thus far. However, he is your son and we respect, as always, both your need to see him and the boy's need to know his family. Therefore, as planned, and God willing, we will arrive on April 30 to spend the Independence Day holiday with you all in the capital. We will stay for three days.

Respectfully,
Miss Laura Emerson and Mrs. Anna Wimble, R.N.

These letters warmed our hearts every time we received them. But we all still wondered whether this arrangement was the right thing – to leave our own flesh and blood in the care of American strangers – not even our people. But they were such good people.

The very deep and secret truth we never talked about was that I, and I think all of us, felt relief at not caring for this last baby of my mother's. This is so shameful to admit… I know *Papá* felt this way. It's a terrible thing to say, but it's true. In the beginning months after *Mamá* left us, especially at the *Colegio*, I held on tight to baby Victor. But little by little, I let the mistresses take more and more care of him. He needed that because he was sickly sometimes. But I realize now, that in the beginning I wanted him close to me because he was the last thing *Mamá* held close to her, the last one Mamá spoke to. Holding on to Victor was like holding on to my *Mamá*. But then something happened to me. I had to put *Mamá*'s death behind me so I could concentrate on the other children. I think putting baby Victor in the mistresses' care helped me with this. This is good and bad. I've never known what it is, but it makes me guilty and sad.

Rose
9
Life with Papá – The Lost Boys Palmas Military Academy and Puerto Rey School of Law, 1920–1925

It was impossible to be his son. It was an ordeal to be his daughter. My father, General Bernardo Beltrán, felt neither deep affection nor dislike for his children, simply the responsibility given to him as a man—to care for us as best he could. *Papá* viewed us, his six children, as small bundles of potential whose will and goals were to be sculpted by him. This was his job, to form us before we were waylaid by our own desires. He put so much of his own will into this task. But, in the end, we children discovered ourselves far away from him, some of us taking twisted paths to finally arrive at our own natures. The General never understood that a growing self cannot be molded into submission. The saddest and most bitter outcomes of *Papá's* child-rearing method, were the lives of two of his boys, Dio–Dionysus, the middle brother and the oldest brother, Milo–Manuel.

Remember my telling you about Dio's naughty behavior at the boarding school with the mistresses? Dio moved far, far beyond his funny bird sounds to make others laugh. His naughtiness never stopped; in fact, it got worse, so when it was time for all of us to come home, the mistresses recommended Dio stay at the school until he was more under control. They knew about something called "child psychology." They said Dio was naughty because his *Mamá* died and he was angry with her. So, he didn't care about breaking rules or acting crazy. But no, *Papá* wanted his boy home. It was enough that the mistresses were already raising the one child, baby Victor.

During our homecoming time from the *Colegio*, we all tried to be on pretty good behavior, especially because *Tía* Teresa was around. But Dio did the strangest things—obvious things that would get anyone in trouble. He came home late in the middle of dinner, rumpled and dirty from doing we didn't know what. One Sunday, everyone was relaxing after church and reading the paper on the front porch. We heard Dio laughing and laughing as he came through the house. He showed up on the porch giggling, wearing one of Patti's flowery dresses and red shoes. Our father stood up and right there took off his belt. Gripping Dio by the elbow with one hand, he struck him on the legs twice.

"Don't you ever, ever put on your sister's clothes. Do you hear me, you devil child. You're just asking to be sent away. Do you hear me?"

"Yes *Papá*," whimpered Dio, as two red welts began to throb on his legs.

I didn't know if that brother of mine was in his right mind. Did he want to provoke *Papá*? Because all the things he did were so unusual.

And that wasn't all, there were stories about him in the neighborhood, that he got old bums to buy him rum. Dio was easy to spot because outside of the house, he wore his straw skimmer with the black band. His look was not complete without tilting that hat slightly to the right. Looking into the front hall mirror every time he left the house, he murmured to no one and everyone, "*Hola, guapo.*" (Hi, good-looking.) Cute, but not cute, as his ways became more and more outrageous.

Drinking in public and playing his guitar in the plaza was the very last straw for *Papá*. On Dio's sixteenth birthday, he was a tall and handsome adolescent. The whole family and our godmother, Lola, gathered to celebrate on the back porch. Dio wore a suit, a white shirt and a blue tie with little diamond shapes that *Papá* had just given him for a gift—a manly present, I guess. We were all laughing and talking at once, loving the delicious strawberry torta. Dio attacked it first, taking a fistful and licking it like a puppy, making us all laugh even harder, until *Papá* reprimands, "*¿Muchacho, que haces? ¡Coje el tenedor!*" (What are you doing, boy? Use your fork!)

That was it. The mood changed. *Papá* sat rocking himself with a long face, not looking at anyone, especially not Dio. After finishing his cake, Dio excused himself to wash his hands and left the room. Five minutes, fifteen minutes passed. Where was he? We called and looked for him. Dio was gone, out of the house, and we were afraid because this was going to make *Papá* go out of his mind.

I fibbed to our father and said, "Dio's friends came to get him; he said to tell you goodbye and thank you for his birthday."

Papá's face was even worse now, scrunching his eyebrows as if he was thinking hard about the boy.

Dio did not come home for dinner or our bedtime. We all finally turned in but no one could sleep. Our bedroom doors were a little bit open so we could hear *Papá's* movements through the house. He was in his study smoking, smoking like crazy, the way he did when he had a problem. The whole house stunk. Sometime close to midnight, we heard *Papá* call to the kitchen part of the house, "*Israel, ven conmigo.*" (come with me).

Israel, who never slept, came running. By the slam of the front door, we knew the two men had left to look for our brother. In the morning, we still didn't know what was going on.

Not being sure about *Papá's* state of mind or wanting to bump into him, I tiptoed down the stairs to the kitchen. Tita was making our breakfast as she had, every day of our lives. With her big eyes, she looked and pointed toward the horse stable in the back yard. Before I could even ask what she meant, *Papá* stormed in and silently gulped down a *café*. He left the house and didn't return until late that night.

Tita grabbed my arm and we ran to the stable in the back. In one of the bolted horse stalls was Dio, clearly hung over and sleeping off last night's rum. We brought him food and juice and questions about what happened.

"I was just celebrating my birthday, *hombre* (man). The old man got so upset. He and Israel came to get me and dragged me home by the arms. I threw up all over *Papà's* American shoes. Ha, ha, ha. They took my guitar and smashed it. I was in really good form last night, too. You should've seen the guys that came to sing with me. *Papá* is an old bull. He says he might throw me out."

We just listened and stared at him through the stall bars. Do you believe he still had on his new birthday tie and fancy hat? I was really worried. I think he pushed *Papá* too far this time.

The next morning was Monday, a school day. We had our routine of eating breakfast at eight a.m. before rushing out to the one-mile walk to school. But the house was quiet. No *Papá*. No Dio; we checked the stable. Tita looked like she was going to explode. In tears, she finally said "He's gone, Dio's gone. The General took him this morning, with a packed suitcase, to a military school, in Palmas, I think. Those places are so strict, like the army."

No one spoke until Milo, our eldest brother, said meekly, "Did he say anything about sending me?"

We were all in shock. Like scared rabbits we got our books and walked to school without saying a word. Something very bad was happening.

Papá was home when we returned from school in the afternoon. He didn't look any of us straight in the eye, and no one dared say anything to him. But he knew that we knew where he had taken Dio. I tell you, this is something my father did, that put another nail in the coffin of our relationship. The very first nail was when he pressured *Mamá* and the new baby to go into hiding with him. Dio would never ever have been treated like this if our mother was here with us.

But, you know, our boy Dio was definitely mixed up. Yes, Dio was as upset about *Mamá's* death as all of us were. But I've always believed – and I'm scared to say this – that a part of him wanted to be, to be... a girl—yes, a girl. All that time he spent when he was a little boy, with the little girls... we all thought he was being a cute little lover boy. It wasn't that! It was that he wanted to *be* like them. One day, I went to pick him up at his friend Susie's house. I was a little early. I found the two in the mother's bathroom putting on lipstick and perfume. Dio had red, red lips that he immediately tried to wipe when he saw me. He wanted to do what women did; he had always been my companion when I took Lola's sewing lessons. He knew how to work the sewing machine and cut fabrics as well as I did. This is what made my brother nervous and confused. This is why he was fresh and funny – to cover everything up. That's what I believed about my brother.

Anyway, going back to those first days of Dio being sent away, I'll tell you that the entire household was *en duelo* (in mourning)... *Papá* didn't have dinner with us on most evenings, preferring to be served some soup in his study—*Tía* Teresa always kept some *caldo de pollo* (chicken soup) going for him. Sometimes, we heard her comforting *Papá,* saying things like, "You did the right thing;" or "It was the only thing you could do. You're a father."

What was most scary was not knowing exactly what *Papá* had planned for his son. Was it forever? Was it just a school? Was it something worse? *Papá* did seem a little sorry. I even started to quietly ask around with family friends. Finally, about a month after Dio was taken away, I got a letter, addressed personally to me without a return address. It was from Dio.

Dearest Rosa and all of you niños (children),

I hope this letter finds you well and in good health. I'm in a terrible place—the Palmas Military Academy. It's supposed to be a military school for boys, but it's really like a prison. The school is very far away from the capital. How could Papá send me here? I'll never, ever, ever speak to him again. It's that place where two students died—they say from maltreatment. I'm not sure that's true, but I'm scared because they are really severe with me. The second day I already had some friends. You know me. Well, they punished me for that, for laughing with the guys at dinner. The next night, we were only whispering together, when the sargento (sargeant) of the dining hall yanks me off the bench. He drags me outside, then takes me through two dark hallways and throws me into a single room with just a low bed and a desk. He yells, "Two days, school only, no outdoors." I don't even know what I did! Ten minutes later, he opens the door with his big key and throws all my belongings into the room. "Beltrán," he says. "We're watching you, you little maricón (fag)."

I don't want you to read most of this letter to the little girls. It's too much for Patti and Nina to hear. Just read them the funny parts, like about the principal major. He's a pig. He wears his green uniform and chest medals when the parents come to visit. But the rest of the time, he walks around the school in his white undershirt and baggy pants, farting down the halls. Tell the kids about how the school looks like a real fort from the distance, with turrets and a drawbridge. The day Papá brought me to the place, even he saluted the soldiers at the front gate.

Rosie, I want to cooperate because I want to go home. But I don't know how I can make it. I know Papá paid for a full year. I'm not going to tell you the stories I've heard about what happens here because I don't want you to worry too much. But if these things turn out to be true, I'm going to run away. Definitely. Don't tell this part to the girls either.

I'll always tell YOU where I am.

Your loving brother, Dio

PS: Take care of my hat. Papá yanked it off me the morning we left, screaming "Carajo, carajo!" (Damn it, damn it!) Then he threw it. It's probably under the front porch.

My brother, Dio, remained at the military academy for almost two years; then he ran away and was lost for a time. He had come home for Christmas twice, always begging, crying to not be sent back to school. *Papá* was firm that he stay through high school graduation. This was like death for the boy, and a slow, sad poisoning for our father. Dio's imprisonment in military school was the result of *Papá*'s beginning to understand the truth about his middle son's natural way of being. This was a bitter pill for *Papá* to swallow.

But our father was to choke on yet another turn in the life of one of his boys: his oldest son, Manuel—Milo, as we affectionately called him.

Like his *Papá,* Milo possessed the same tall, lanky frame and cinnamon brown coloring. We children teased Milo about his long rubbery arms—arms that ended in the largest hands you ever saw. He was proud of his paws, though, because they were the magic that let him pitch perfect balls.

Papá hated Milo's love for everything baseball. The General preferred to put his big boy to work, doing more productive things. So, Milo pulled tree trunks and wielded a machete in the fields as well as any of the hired workers at our farm. Never should any of the General's boys feel entitled because of the position they had been born into. If Milo bristled at this treatment, you would never know, because being a boy of few words, when he was free, he usually snuck away to a corner of the house or outdoors, to satisfy his second passion: devouring endless books of history. When *Papá* barked one of his demands in his usual gruff tone, Milo would simply slide his lanky frame toward his new task.

In the spring of Milo's senior year in high school, our father announced at dinner one night, "Milo will be enrolled in the Puerto Rey School of Law this fall to study *derecho* (law). He will finish in three years and then join our political party—a man like that will help our cause."

This was a good number of years after our mother's death, and we were then older children sitting around the table with our mouths wide open, watching for a sign from poor Milo. He turned white; he was horrified; never had he expressed any interest in the law. Lowering his head, he slowly digested the dictatorial edict that had just been levied upon him.

Sixty days later, my brother was driven to the university campus and we were only to see him subsequently on holidays. I missed him terribly, because he and I were the oldest, the *jefes,* bosses of the children; putting our heads together to figure out what *Papá* and his schemes were up to. It was clear that our father was a shrewd wheeler-dealer, always in cahoots with cronies who either engaged his politics or his money. It was Milo and I who were the "lookouts". I guess we assumed that role after our mother died. While she was proud and encouraging of her husband, *Mamá* was also wary of some of his judgments. Milo and I could never tell our father what to do, but we could at least foresee an oncoming blow. Like the time we all started school late because *Papá* lost our tuition money in a bad land deal. Or the time he got paid in hundreds of cases of Coca-Cola, instead of cash, when he lent the Americans money for a new soda factory that failed.

In any case, I was now on my own without Milo, trying to keep my eyes open as best I could. My brother kept in touch by regular letters written in his fine cursive hand. He told me of the boredom of his classes, and how the logical tracks of his legal texts were particularly easy for him to understand. He was doing well and following *Papá's* demands with the same dogged loyalty. I worried about this boy; where was his own *coraje,* (courage)? When was he going to grow a pair? He insisted everything would be okay for him in the end. "Don't worry, Rosie," he said. "I know what I'm doing."

Following the custom of the times, students boarded with families in the surrounding area. So, Milo went to stay with the Medinas, a family who grew to love him as a son. The Medinas lived on the outskirts of the town, barely making their own living from vegetable farming. But what they lacked in comforts, they possessed in good nature as they showered Milo with the best sleeping quarters, sheets, soap, food and coffee, they had to offer. They were honored to have an educated young man from the capital city of Catalina with them, and they spared nothing to make him feel at home. "You are our blessing," Señora Medina often said. Neighbors from the area would shyly appear to gawk at the tall, handsome almost-lawyer in their midst. The boldest of them might ask Milo to read a letter or an onerous municipal notice they had received in the mail. Yes, in the 1920s, this was an illiterate community with barely a schoolhouse or educational tradition to speak of among its poor majority. Milo was as moved by these conditions as he was by the deep and growing affection of the Medinas. He wrote, "Are these strangers filling the hole that opened in me after *Mamá's* death?"

Milo came home for both *Navidad*, Christmas, and summer holidays after his first year. But at the end of his second year, something happened to arouse him from the somnambulist's sleep he had been living in up to then. He began to question his movements. He didn't want to go home that next summer, but to stay in the University's town. He also wanted to spend more time with the Medinas' daughter, Fernanda, who he had been courting on the weekends. He asked himself, "Could this be love?"

So, with a firm tone and exquisite logic, he wrote to *Papá* telling him he would not be home that summer; he had gained employment in the local area for the season; and that given his receipt of first prize that year for constitutional law, he was clearly in firm command of his studies. The letter was a statement of fact, of intent. It was not the letter of a young man asking any sort of permission from his father. It was the latter that steamed our father the most. He was losing his iron grip on his oldest son.

Papá was in a terrible mood all that summer. We stayed out of his way and gave him no hint of trouble, lest he thunder with the force of his injured paternal pride. We held our breaths until the official word that Milo had started his third and last year of law school. He pursued his last courses with great success, maintaining his top five per cent ranking. But three months before graduation, Milo detonated an absolute bomb: he withdrew from Law School. He stated simply in a formal letter to the dean that the law no longer held his interests.

Milo never sat for his final exams. He married Fernanda the following year, with only me, his big sister, in attendance. Making his home with his wife and true love, he immediately took on the position of a schoolteacher in the rural area's one-room schoolhouse. In the evenings, Fernanda served *tasitas de café* (cups of coffee), as *el profesor* read and wrote letters for his neighbors.

Papá had lost another son.

Rose
10
Fat Feet Walks in
Catalina, Puerto Rey, Late 1920s

As the years passed, the cold pit that lived in my stomach after my mother's death began to disappear. The children were growing; they were at least physically healthy; and hadn't died yet from some mysterious disease. I was the *big-sister-mother*. We only had each other and I knew my duty. I loved them and resented them; adored them and resented them. Some of the children troubled me, though, as I've started to describe, from what I'll call the "mental" side.

I haven't told you yet about Nina, our angelic one, who spoke little and walked on a cloud. Her full name, Nina Maria, gave a lightness to this complicated little girl's spirit. She possessed, what I'll call, some interesting talents. By age twelve, she had taught herself English and French and spoke them fluently to anyone who listened. But ask her in her native Spanish what she wanted for breakfast or how school was that day, and she would be mute!

Nina could go a whole day without talking. In the time it took her to use the bathroom potty, she counted the tiles on the wall, categorizing them by color and imperfections. And at night, it was her job to follow the stars and constellations above our island. If she wasn't tucked in her bed after lights out, I found her sitting solemnly on the dark front steps, gazing up at the sky.

"Not yet, Rosie," she whined, as I dragged her into the house. "Orion is glowing in the full moon, and I have to see it."

Papá finally consulted a neurologist to examine Nina. The doctor told him the little girl was either a *savant* or moving toward the crash of a mental illness. *Papá* refused to pay the doctor for this ridiculous diagnoses, grumbling that all he needed to do was get the child on the correct life course. "Oh *Papá,*" I thought to myself, "will you ever understand any of us?"

When I could manage to stop worrying about the children for a while, I turned to myself. By the age of eighteen, I knew that I was pretty and smart. For the style of those days, I may even have been considered luscious—with a large soft bosom, round hips, and a tiny waist to show it all off. Best of all, I had a forward mind and quick tongue—well trained by *Mamá* and refined by the years spent overseeing our family of children.

I knew I caught the attention of both men and boys. But as the General's daughter, they only nodded their respectful hellos as they glanced my way, instead of muttering the ridiculous *piropos* (cat whistles) so commonly heard from Latin men. *"¡Hola bella!"* (Hi gorgeous!) Yes, I knew all the gossip about who might finally land me in marriage. I was considered a catch given my own charms, and the influence of my father, of course. I know what you're thinking, and I won't deny it: that I inherited some of our father's arrogance.

I led a strange double life at this time. On the one hand, I ran the household with *Tía* Teresa, organized the accounts for *Papá's* ever-changing projects, and functioned as the little mother. On the other hand, I dreamed big dreams fired by the glamour and money-making know-how of America. Hollywood movies made the rounds in our city, and I saw them all. There were beautifully dressed women, gallant men in fedora hats, people speaking their minds, and the likes of Hedy Lamarr, Claudette Colbert and Rudolf Valentino. I loved the clothes. I had a great eye and was quick at designing patterns in my head, thanks to Lola's tailoring lessons. Roaming the shops on *Avenida Dorada* for imported fabrics, I made my dresses to copy the American styles. I imagined myself in New York City wearing high pumps and a coat with a fox collar, elegantly clicking my heels all the way to my Park Avenue office. What a dream!

With bobbed hair one year, and a finger-wave the next, you could say I was ready for "something," but what? Love had not struck me yet. I didn't know how to do that. While *Mamá's* loss was hurting less, I was still always tense. Like I needed to be on constant watch. Was it the younger ones who got on my nerves? Was it worry about *Papá's* next crazy idea or business deal? Or was it terror about where my own life would land?

But I forgot to tell you this part: around this time, *Papá* was quite a force to contend with. He had finally recovered from the depression and fury over our brother Milo's betrayal. But there was a drivenness to him now. He scheduled meeting after meeting with groups of men at our home. He boasted to them about his job as an undersecretary in the President's cabinet, his influence with the current government, his urban development projects in the countryside and all his other kudos. What a character! Not a humble bone in his body. This man was up to something, it was big, and I think it had to do with lots of money. What I didn't know was that I was going to be a pawn in this developing plan.

One evening, having just turned eighteen, I was called into *Papá's* study. "Oh no, now, what does he want?" I knocked and entered the foul cloud of cigar smoke that took my breath away. The ceiling fans whirled the stinking stuff in grey ribbons all over the room. I hated that smell in my hair! But I managed to smile politely at my father.

There was a gentleman visitor present, who after making a little startled jump in his chair, immediately began to stand in greeting. *Papá* also stood and formally introduced me to the gentleman.

"Señor Manuel Goya, may I present my precious elder daughter, Señorita Rosina Dorada Burgos Beltrán."

I nodded with the proper lowered eyes, inspecting the man's bunion–bulging shoes while my eyeballs were down there. Fat, ugly feet for sure! I almost giggled. Then Fat Feet actually took my hand and courteously kissed it.

The giggles spilled over, and I tried to cover them up with a cough and a *perdóneme* (excuse me).

Mr. Goya wore the usual gentleman's summer uniform of white linen suit and bowtie, but his shirt was rumpled and perspired. His heavy eyelids and drooping shoulders made him look like an old man. I already knew Goya was a widower and a businessman who owned stores in several cities. I'd seen the respectful attitude other men had toward him. There was also something about his opinions on Puerto Rey politics being in the newspaper. Funny how at that moment I remembered *Mamá* and her canasta ladies snickering on the porch about the bountiful seeds this man had planted in feminine flowers all over Catalina. I had no idea what that meant until then. Goya pretended to have never seen me before, but I knew well that he was one of *Papá*'s colleagues who stole looks at my bosom, when I served the men coffees in the study.

Papá suddenly said, "I'm so pleased to have introduced you both. Rosa, Mr. Goya will be coming by this Wednesday to take us out to dinner—just the three of us. And you, *mi hija* (my daughter), are the special guest." What was he talking about? I nodded my goodbyes and stumbled out of the room, nervous about what had just happened. I wouldn't be able to make any sense of it until I was alone in bed that night.

Tita, who was dozing in the hallway chair, ready to serve the gentlemen more cold drinks, heard the study door click close and came to me. *"¿Señorita, señorita Rosa, pero que pasa? Estas pálida y sudada."* (Señorita Rosa, what's wrong? You're pale and perspired.) She took my hand and it was cold. "Did your father scold you again?"

"No... no... I just don't feel well... It was the stinking smoke, I think. I'm just going to bed."

I walked into the calm of my room, lit by the pink lamp on my vanity. I stood for a long time in front of the large round mirror and studied myself. I think I was in a trance. I liked the way my shape, my height and my clothes, all went together. And my face: it was bright and intelligent. *Mamá* told me I'd turn out this way, but I never believed her. I started to undress and began to cry a little as I stood there in my lacy slip. I looked at my reflection again, when a sob from the pit of my stomach let go.

"What... what... oh God, oh God... I know what this is." Standing in the shadow of the night lamp, I suddenly saw what the men saw and what Goya and *Papá* saw. "*Papá, Papá*, oh my God... I understand... *un arreglo* (an arrangement) with Goya. *Papá* wants to marry me to him—a marriage arrangement... "

I fell on the bed. I don't remember if I fainted, screamed, gagged—but I knew I never felt such rage come out of me. I cried and yelled and cried. And talked and talked and talked to myself all night. I had never even been in love! Besides a few little kisses at parties and a walk in the square with so-and-so who touched my hand, that was it. From the outside... I guess I looked like a woman, but on the inside, I was a crazy cave of feelings, and the private parts of my body were mysterious for sure. I might as well have been my silly little sisters, who didn't even know they were women!

I knew about these arrangements. I had heard about them. Why did *Papá* want to marry me off to this old man? For his money? I didn't think he was the richest. *Papá* has made money too, but you know what? He's lost it and wasted it. And besides, there's always that embarrassing thing about his reputation: Ha, the rebel General whose coup flopped! What an ass!

"*Mamá,* why aren't you here? This would never be happening to me if you were here. What's going to happen to my life? What am I supposed to do? This can't be normal? It can't be, with an old man like Goya! *Papá i*s a cannibal. I bet he's selling me, selling me to Goya for some kind of deal, some kind of money. I know him. No, this can't be happening, no… "

I grabbed my Bible, my mother's Bible, and looked for I didn't know what. Wiping my eyes, I found the Psalms Estrella loved and the piece about choosing paths that lie before you. The book fell out of my hands and onto the floor as I found some sleep.

At about six a.m. the sun began to peek through my bedroom windows. Streaks of pale light streamed through the lacy curtains hung by my mother many years ago.

"How did it get to be morning? I must have slept." Feeling the ache in my stomach, I sat bolt upright. "After last night, I don't even know how I can be alive right now." I saw my crumpled pillow smeared with make-up and tears and stumbled to the commode and then to the porcelain basin, to wash my face. "Oh no, my face is a red, round tomato smeared in mascara, and my neck is full of that bumpy rash I get every time I go to sleep crying."

I couldn't bear to look at myself. I washed, put on a clean nightgown, turned over my pillow and sank back into bed. Really awake now, I saw the sun shining over the backyard garden, which we called the orchid jungle. Finally, the full sun splashed against my windows, bathing the room with the light that took my breath away every morning. "But this wasn't a regular morning, it was the first day of looking for my own path."

Papá's plans for me made me ill. When I thought of Goya, I felt nauseous and panicked. I wanted to cry all over again, but no, I stopped myself. I knew this feeling wouldn't go away, but I had to control it. In an American magazine, I read that you could restrain yourself from acting on a feeling even though it still lived inside you.

Tita gently knocked on the door—always the first one up. "Rosie, you look terrible, *hija* (daughter). What can I do for you?"

I had the presence of mind to tell her it was my cycle, with terrible cramps. "Tell *Papá*, I'll be in bed all day, and would you please bring me some of your oregano tea?" Ugh, even though I hated it.

Tita dutifully told *Papá* about my feminine condition. He respected that and knew better than to disturb me. That always worked. But around lunchtime, he sent in a message with Tita wishing me better and sincerely hoping I would be *lista* (ready), tip-top, and looking gorgeous for our Wednesday dinner with Goya. I began to sob all over again, almost vomiting the tea. But from a quiet corner of my mind, I saw the image of my godmother, Lola, my confidante, and my angel since *Mamá's* death. I called Tita and told her to ask Lola if she could meet me in the backyard that afternoon. "I'm not alone, I'm not alone. I'm not alone," I told myself. Lola would know what to do.

Eventually I got out of bed and went to the orchid garden to wait for Lola. Sitting on the green wicker divan I might have looked calm, but I was screaming inside. I watched a perky male hummingbird in a busy dance, buzzing its way to a red orchid. The bird was drinking from the flower, when one of the iguanas from our garden began to climb the orchid's stem. The gallant little bird was scared off. The shiny reptile with its pudgy, clawed feet tore some petals along its climb. "Ugh ugh, the fat feet… And what was it doing now? Oh God, it was licking the orchid petals with its long slimy tongue, darting in and out like… like… no… no, you stop it!"

I threw one slipper, then the next, then my glass of water, then my book. "I'll throw the chair at you if I have to. Get out, out!"

By this time Tita was running to the garden to see what was going on, saying, *"¿Señorita, señorita Rosie, que pasa?"* (What's the matter?)

I responded, *"No se, no se, estoy loca. Un bicho me asustó. Búscame a la Lola. ahora!"* (I don't know what's wrong with me. I'm insane. A creature scared me. Get me Lola, right now!)

Lola didn't come until evening. I was a zombie by that time, still in my nightgown and not even able to tolerate the lamplight in my room. I had crawled back into bed with a face that looked like a tomato and an expression that said: "It's the end of the world." When tiny Lola finally knocked and entered, she was saying, "I know, I know all about it. Your father pulled me into his study and gave me the news: Manuel Goya has asked for your hand."

I screamed like a howling cat and she ran to cover my mouth. My godmother listened to my litany of anguish and rage at my father. "How could he? I know it's about money. He's sold me like an Indian rug or a sack of rice. I heard them talking once about Goya supporting *Papá's* party candidate for president. Traitor, cannibal, my own father. Who will take care of the children if I have to live with the old man? And what about being in love? I'm running away and taking the children with me."

"Darling, think of what you're saying," says Lola. "How would you all live?"

An hour must have gone by as Lola listened, soothed, and wisely smiled at every crazy plan of escape I came up with. "Calm down now and listen to what I'm thinking. You know, this may not be as terrible as you think. I know, I know. He's old for you, and you certainly don't love or even know him. But the way to look at this is like a business arrangement where many people can benefit – primarily yourself. He's a businessman, right? Well, your father says Goya would put you to work, probably running his business accounts. He knows about your cleverness with numbers. What would be more satisfying to him than to put his trustworthy wife in charge of his books? Think of it, Rosie: he'll pay you a salary and who knows, a little wiggle here and a little wiggle there of the books might make you a very rich girl."

"And then, I can run away with the children," I blurted out.

"Well… yes, if that's what you want to do in a few years," says Lola.

"But here's what I'm thinking, *hija* (daughter). You know, marriage arrangements like this are made a lot in our country. In my experience, marriages for real love are hardly ever a success. Think of it. You'll want for nothing. You enter his beautiful home here in the old city. You'll be a lady, you'll have servants. Goya is known to be a kind and generous man to his women; the only problem is that he has too many of them! But his legal wife is the queen and he's only had one other. She died a few years ago and left him a widower."

I listened. I was finished crying for now, but my body was exhausted.

Rose, the General's Daughter, at the time of
her arranged marriage. Age 18

"Stay in bed for the next day or two," said Lola, giving me a squeeze. "I'll come every day to talk with you, but by Wednesday evening, you'll need to be ready and looking like your gorgeous self. It's an important night for you—don't think about your *Papá's* end of it anymore. He is who he is. Now you must be smart and business-like for yourself. Someday, real love will happen, you'll see. By then, you'll be a strong and powerful lady, running your own life. And who knows, maybe the love will turn out to be... What did you call Goya, Fat Feet, himself?"

"No, no, no," I screamed and laughed at the same time, throwing a pillow at little Lola, as she slipped out the door.

Rose
11
The Census Takers
Las Piedras, Puerto Rey, Late 1920s

I'm ashamed to talk about this part of my life. I went against my heart and my will and agreed to marry a man unknown to me, someone I am far, far away from loving. I was intimate with him, smiled, and was mostly pleasant, all the time thinking about how I could get away. I planned to save all the money I could. My goal: to leave my husband and become my own person. I was going to America, and taking the girls, Patti and Nina, with me.

I was furious with my father. I didn't think that would ever go away. He used me for his own business benefit. My marriage to Goya, plain and simple, guaranteed my husband's contribution to *Papá*'s new political party, and the candidates they wanted to bring forward for election. And *Papá* was not stopping with me. Patti and Nina would be the next puppets in his schemes, as they suffered daily under the stiff collar of daughterly duties demanded of them. Little feels like love in a paternal dictatorship.

Despite all of *Papá's* restrictions, my sisters had grown and matured quickly in the short period after my marriage. From their high school baccalaureates, they went into the Teachers' College, hoping that the end of their studies would mark some change of status in the eyes of *Papá:* from girls to very well-equipped young women. But this was unlikely.

To make everything worse, real social fun was hard for them to come by, and young men were almost impossible to meet, as *Papá* insisted on a chaperone accompanying them to every party and gathering. What the General was doing was imprisoning the girls while looking for good marriage arrangements to benefit *him.* Love and friendship, never mind. My sisters struggled to stay cheerful and hopeful about their lives, and I worked at keeping them positive. Our secret was that I would have them "over to my house" as much as I could, so that they could go out on their own for an evening or meet people who came to visit our home.

In the summer of 1928, the following article appeared in a main Puerto Rey newspaper, announcing plans for major developments in rural parts of our country:

Catalina, Puerto Rey, June 27, 1928: *The esteemed President of Puerto Rey announces a multi-level plan of development that includes the building of public schools in five townships; the cutting of main roads in the central region of the country to connect local byways with the city; and the surveying of the country's population Census. The President intends to reach these goals within an intense and productive period of five years.*

I want to tell you about this summer because it marks the important point where my sisters decided to form their *own* life plans outside the designs set for them by *Papá*. The General imposed a severe demand on the girls: they were to live and work for the summer as government Census Takers in the sweltering, dry and rocky Las Piedras province of our country.

As one of several undersecretaries now in the President's Cabinet, the General's charge was to organize a team that would conduct the population Census. Many people were hired and trained for the project. As always, *Papá* tried to recruit all of his now adult children into the enterprise, as well as anyone else who owed him even the whisper of a favor.

When he asked me to volunteer, I gave him a flat out, "No. Don't you understand I'm running a household and my husband's stores now? Isn't that what you wanted from me? Definitely not!"

But Patti and Nina's sweaty chore was set. Traveling on horseback, they were to accompany the local mayor with big Census ledgers, recording every person, chicken, horse, goat and mule that lived in every house, barn, shack, lean-to and cave in the rural region of Las Piedras. This was an area with large farms and rocky hills that would be hard to cross by car. The girls begged not to be sent to this place alone. But *Papá* insisted it was their duty and an honor to work for the progress of the country. They would be riding side-saddle, which meant wearing ugly skirts wide enough to swing a leg over the saddle pommel.

Patti grumbled: "No double stirrups or riding pants for us. Young ladies do not open their legs on horses," she mocked. "It's the 1920s for God's sake!"

The only excitement in all this was that the inexperienced girls were actually government officials with badges now, not to mention educated *señoritas*. They were offered a *respeto* (respect) they had never experienced before. And boy, did they take advantage of that! Over the years, Patti told me the story of that summer, many times:

Papá arranged for us to be boarders on the Santana family farm. The Santanas were modest, soft-spoken campesinos (farm family) who ran a goat farm in a little green valley of the generally dusty region. When we first saw our quarters, la casita de atrás (the little house in the back) looked cute as a button. You could tell the flowery quilts on the twin beds were brand new, and that the crisp organdy curtains had just been hung. There was a radio, and a coqueta (vanity table) with a round mirror and bench.

"We'll definitely fight over that," I said to Nina.

"Oh, who cares," answered Nina, cool and aloof as usual. "I brought plenty of books to read."

I drew back the curtains at the back window and smiled at the deep valley that lay beyond. Then I noticed some goat pens about forty yards away. "There's a Nubian pen, the goats with long dog ears. There's a Saanen pen too—those milk goats with the pretty horns, and... What's that awful smell?"

"What smell?" asked Nina.

"The stink, the goat stink!"

I started to get mad. "Oh God. Tú sabes que? (You know what?) This casita was probably a goat shack! Disgusting. It stinks like goat poo. We are not staying here. Come on, get your things, we'll tell them we're leaving." Oh boy, Patti was usually quiet and calm, but if something really, really bothered her, she could make a great big fuss. So, Patti called out, "Señor Santana, Señor Santanaaaa..."

Mr. Santana was outside and responded, "Señoritas, señoritas, que pasa? Calma." (Young ladies, what's wrong? Calm down.)

Patti was a fright with her blouse untucked and her hair in a mess. "Señor, you have put us in a goat shack. How could you do that? Do you know who our father is?"

Nina whispered calmly into Patti's hot ear that it was Father himself who made the arrangements. "Oh... Well, well, we can't stay here..."

"Señoritas, please, I have an idea. Freshen yourselves, then come over to the main house. Dinner is almost ready, and while you eat, my wife, Ancha will freshen the casita. Of course, the casita was never a goat shack. What an idea! You're just smelling the evening breeze, that's el sereno (the night air). Around here, we like to say that Las Piedras stirs its aromas before sunset so we know what tomorrow will bring. The goat smell tonight? That means we'll finally have rain in the morning."

The girls looked at each other, rolling their eyeballs, and mumbling something about the "hillbilly weatherman."

Rain, rain, and more rain. The girls woke the next morning to one of the biggest downpours they had ever seen. The valley below had disappeared in the mist, cool air now replaced the scorching heat, and the puddles to get from the casita to the main house were the size of ponds.

"Good morning, honored Señoritas," grinned the self-satisfied Mr. Santana. "How do you like our weather?" he sing-songed.

The girls were fuming, and before they could even begin to hope for canceling the first Census-taking day on account of rain, they spotted gear on the porch that was obviously meant for their first day of work: enormous rain ponchos, rubber boots and hefty saddle bags carrying the big Census ledgers.

"We're sunk," groaned Nina.

At that moment, out of the Santanas' house came the mayor who would accompany the girls on their rounds. Mr. Santana introduced el Alcalde Rubiroso Murillo, who courteously extended his hand to each young lady, making direct eye contact with their bosoms.

"We're doomed," mumbled Patti, and they all went in for breakfast. "That first workday was unlike anything we had ever experienced in our lives: Heading for the heart of the countryside, we trekked across swollen streams, streets that swallowed the horses' hooves, and

sheets of rain that smacked our cheeks until they were pink. The mayor, with his rifle hidden under his poncho, insisted on riding behind us for supposed safety reasons. But we suspected he either liked the swaying of the horses' behinds, or ours. Aside from his sneaky looks, the man wasn't a problem for us because we had him cornered with our sarcastic smirks, keeping him wondering whether we were laughing at him. But I have to say that when we really needed him, when anyone questioned our business or doubted our small thimble of authority as the girl Census Takers, he came to attention. Rubi, as we called him, neck-reined his horse with one hand. At any sign of trouble, he pulled out his rifle like a saber with his free hand, gently laid it across the front of his saddle, and curled his fingers around the trigger.

Over those long weeks, the daily work was grueling. And then there were the violent shifts in weather. We either baked in the scorching heat or bathed in torrential downpours. We learned the drill quickly: a reception of mean, barking dogs usually greeted us at the entrance of every finca (farm). The dogs called the farm foreman, and the foreman called the patrón, the boss. Rubi always spoke first, introducing us and the purpose of our visit. He was the mayor, after all, well known by his people as a no-nonsense kind of guy, and the weapon on his saddle reminded them of this.

In preparation for our job, we had practiced the Census questions for months, learning to lower our squeaky girl voices to sound older and more in command.

We recorded the names, ages, schooling and occupations of everyone who lived on a farm. Then we asked about the farm's acreage, livestock and number of people who were hired workers. These were touchy questions because every owner was required to register his laborers and show proof of salaries paid. Like clockwork, at this point in the interview, we Census Takers were invited to come out of the sun and have a cold drink. So, under the shade of a tree, numbers were squeezed out of the nervous and sweating patrón.

This was when Nina's dreamy self, came in handy. She innocently got up and wandered the barns and sheds. She loved counting pigs, chickens, and every baby animal she could find. If a farmer was warned about our visit ahead of time, the baby animals would often be hidden so as not to be counted as livestock. "Remember", said Patti, "the Census also sets tax rates for a farm." Nina was very good at this—she could find anything that moved. One day, she rejoined the group, carrying a half dozen piglets in her big skirt. "Look what I found hiding in a toolbox, cochinitos (piglets), and there are so many more!" The farmer sat sweating in his place.

After the barn inspections, came the hard part. Each of us was armed with heavy binoculars and trained our eyepieces on a specific segment of pastureland—counting the number of grazing critters: twenty-one bulls, sixteen horses, twenty-two chivos (goats)…

Nina started to squeal one day, "Patti, Patti, come here, what are these, chivitos (baby goats)?"

I looked through my sister's binoculars, and high on the ridge of the main pasture was a stand of many trees, kind of like a little forest, and romping in front were little ones. "I think those are children, let's go see."

Rubi came to life on hearing this and mumbled, "Wait, I have something important to give you young ladies, I forgot about this." He took a manila envelope out of his saddle bag and gave it to us. The envelope was addressed to us in our father's handwriting. The note inside said simply, "Always look just beyond a finca's (farm's) boundaries. You will find a world unto itself. Working people live here. I want you to discover them on your own. They are the uncounted in our country. Que Dios las bendigan. (May God bless you). Papá."

We three riders slowly plodded our way down into the pasture valley. Reaching the flat part, we made our way across the grasses, weaving in and out of cows and calves who stared at us vacantly or baaed as we passed. We rode slowly forward in the hot sun for about half a mile, keeping our sights on the ridge. The incline up to the other side of the valley was long, but thankfully not steep. Our horses were lathered now, and we were all desperate for water. Disregarding Rubi's custom to approach first, we girls moved up ahead, finding four small children who were barely clothed. Rubi was not pleased and firmly called out for who was in charge. A young woman peeked out of a wooden lean-to that was barely standing up against a row of palm trees. Wiping her hands on her skirt, she smiled and asked how she could be of help. The oldest child of about six ran to a brown barrel and scooped out a cup of water, shyly offering it to Nina. She had to bend way down in her saddle to reach the little boy's outstretched arm. When she took the cup, he caressed her hand and ran away. The other children were now running to the water barrel as well, fighting for cups to offer drinks to the visitors.

I gently asked the woman how she lived in this place.

"We belong to, I mean.... work for the patrón, Señorita."

"Does he pay you?" I asked.

"Well, no, he lets us use a little piece of land to grow our food, yuca and beans. We pay him for this."

"How?" I asked.

"Well, we work the full day for him in the fields, or with the animals, until the sun is down."

"Does the patrón take care of you, then?"

"Oh no, señorita," said the woman with a bitter laugh. "If we're hurt or wounded from the work, it's our bad luck. If you look closely along this ridge, there are many families who live in the same miserable way. We try to take care of each other, but our lives are hard."

"How many are here?" I asked.

"Maybe twenty of us."

We now understand the purpose of the last column on the Census ledger page, designated "Others." These are the invisible people: sharecroppers who lived in the shadows of the farm—"beyond the boundaries" as Papá had written. Unpaid, illiterate, and voiceless. Papá would later tell us that these workers lived only to about the age of fifty and almost half of their babies died before their first birthdays.

We were stunned. We filled out the columns in our ledgers, thanked the family for our drinks, and slowly turned our horses for the long, sad, pensive ride across the pasture valley.

Rose
12
Planning Under the Iron Fist
Catalina, Puerto Rey, Early 1930s

When is the twisting of our lives by men going to stop? *Carajo* (damn it)—this shaping of our destinies by their hands has to end, and I'm going to do it! What am I doing with a man who is still a stranger to me and never home? He is intimate with me without feeling and holds me out like a showpiece to run his business. This is no life for me. I'm lonely. I've never been in love. You know what? I'm going to start my own business in America! And my sisters. This is no life for them either. Their business should be to get good jobs, become gorgeous, fall in love, and marry wonderful men.

A corral of wild horses started to move inside me. My plan started with visions of moving to New York, perfecting my English, and owning my own stores. These were not only dreams. In fact, I had just solicited a visa application and contacted my New York cousins for advice on moving there. I'm going. I'm focused.

But there was an unexpected development at home with Goya. I don't know if it was because of the wiggle in my step, the American books and magazines I kept all over the house, or Goya's actual discovery of my visa application to the U.S. in the desk drawer, but one morning over breakfast he suddenly asked, "Are you thinking of going to New York?"

I almost dropped my coffee cup. I had to think fast and answer him. "Well, well, yes, in the way you and I always blah blah blah about moving there and living in a pretty apartment and expanding our business there."

"Well Rosa," he said. "I've actually been thinking over that idea myself and getting advice from a *compadre* (close friend) who lives there."

Hearing this made me burn with rage. This was *my* dream. Go with *him*? I wanted to get away from him! But wait, wait a minute. *Calma,* I told myself. This doesn't have to destroy the plan. I've been told that visas for the U.S. are given much more easily to married couples than to women by themselves. We could establish ourselves and then send for the girls. But *Dios mío* (my God), this was such a gigantic plan. There was *Papá* to tell, making sure the boys would be okay being left here, and so much more. But I was going, damn it. I would deal with my husband in New York. Somehow, I had the feeling that Goya suggested the idea to test me, provoke me. To tell you the truth, I didn't see this man being able to live without his Puerto Reyan comforts and influence on the island.

Around the halfway mark of Patti and Nina's summer job in the countryside as Census Takers, I arranged it so that I had business in the store we owned in that area—I picked up the girls in my car on a Sunday. They were waiting on the porch of their *casita* dressed in their Sunday best. The Santanas, their host family, were out in the front yard gawking at the two princesses sashaying into my new Ford. When we arrived at the little restaurant in town, I saw the strain of the summer job on the girls' appearance. Yes, big smiles and pretty dresses, but their faces and slender hands were burnt from the sun; there were dark circles under their eyes; and I had never seen them so thin. I hated *Papá* at that moment.

After Patti and Nina ate their fill of Caribbean stew and a beautiful flan, they talked incessantly about their days on horseback, visiting big ranches and backyard chicken farms. I told them finally to settle down and hear my news. "We three girls are moving to New York."

"What, what?" they cried.

I totally shocked them and began to roll out my idea. I would go to New York first, get myself organized with a job and a nice place to live, and they both would follow me there in about two years. I saw the disappointment in their faces as the reality sank in that they weren't running away immediately.

We talked and talked about living in America, speaking English every day like smart ladies, and being in business together. The girls swore to finish their teaching internships by the end of the year, and Nina, the brain, even promised to take some extra business and accounting courses that could come in handy later. But what about *Papá*? He must never, never know about this plan. I made the girls swear not to tell a single soul—not even the boys. *Papá* could destroy everything.

"And Rosie," the girls asked. "Does this mean you're running away from your husband too?"

"You leave Goya to me. I know how to handle him." At that point, to tell you the truth, I was faking my courage. I had no idea how this master plan was really going to work.

After coffees and laughing and toasting each other, I finally brought the giddy girls back to the Santanas. There were hugs and kisses and some tears, as Patti and Nina faced another four long weeks on the job. The New York plan would hopefully get them through. After the final good-bye, I drove my car onto the two-lane highway that curved toward our capital city of Catalina. I kept no memory of that ride, as my mind filled with more wild horses than I could handle. First for me and then for the girls. I was going to leave—my country and then my husband. I knew how to do it. Step by step. I had been thinking and planning for this since the day darling *Papá* married me to Goya.

I could imagine the fantastic dreams dreamed by Patti and Nina after our Sunday dinner. Fates have their way of speaking, and so it happened that the following workday struck the girl Census Takers like a lightning bolt. Could their lives be starting to change already?

I understood from Patti that the next day was on the cooler side as distant clouds crept closer to where the riders were moving. As they approached their first farm, a black cat slithered out of the bushes and began to walk along with the riders. Suddenly, claps of thunder shook the sky, and as far as the horses were concerned, shook the ground as well. The terrified cat jumped straight up into the air yowling, and fell down to the ground right in front of Nina's big horse. The horse screeched in terror, reared up on its hind legs, and Nina fell off like a bag of yuca. Smashing her right knee, the poor girl's screams added to the cacophony, announcing that the Census Takers had arrived!

Nina and the rest of the crew were taken into the farmhouse with great courtesy by the farm couple, and the farmer's son was sent on horseback to get the town doctor. It was raining like crazy now. "The boy will take a while," said the *patrón* in his country slang. Then to his wife, "The officials will need a meal." Poor Nina cried as she looked at her obviously broken leg. After it was cleaned and wrapped around a plank, Nina got two heavy shots of Caribbean rum – the best, you know – and slept for hours. Thank goodness.

As they all waited for lunch, and the doctor, and the rain to stop, Mayor Rubie and Patti decided to take the farmer's Census. Why not? Why waste the visit? And Nina, the patient, was unconscious. After the hot meal of goat stew and plantains, the boy and doctor finally arrived, trailing in the wetness of the afternoon. After a small round of rum for courage, they all carried the poor girl into the doctor's mule-drawn ambulance. Nina said her leg didn't hurt at all. She was so drunk. As the group left the farmhouse hugging the generous hosts, Rubie winked at them, pointing to the Census ledger. *"No se apuren por esto, están bien,"* he said. (Don't worry at all about this, you're fine.)

The good luck part of this great hullabaloo was that the doctor wrote an official set of orders saying the girl with the broken leg was not to work for the summer. She was to go back to her home and convalesce there accompanied by her sister. Well, that was that. *Se acabó!* (It was over!)

A week later, after the girls were back to their fresh and clean selves in the city, the convalescing Nina confessed something: that she maybe fell off the horse on purpose. "I could have held on, but I wanted to go home, so I let go of my reins. "Interesting girl," is all I could think…

Once at home in the capital, Patti and Nina set about living their lives with their escape plan hidden inside them. I want to emphasize that at this time, Nina and Patti, both in their twenties, were the only two children left under *Papá's* roof, and thus under his domination. The boys were living their own lives. This was not a good situation for the girls, because they knew it was only a matter of time before the General's crafty mind came up with another way of engaging them in his hungry plans for political involvement and recognition.

A few months later, as graduation from the girls' Teacher's College neared, Patti ran over one morning as

Goya and I were eating breakfast and, with great anguish, told us this story.

"You're not going to believe this new order from our General. Last night in his kindest possible voice, *Papá* announced, *"Niñas, we'll take a stroll in the square tonight. Wear your pretty clothes, I want to show you off, one of you on each arm, walking to the tune of progress for our beloved island republic of Puerto Rey."*

I immediately thought, "Uh oh, this is not going to be good."

Nina said, "Maybe I should do one of my boba tricks. You know, deaf and mute with no expression on my face."

"Little sister, I don't know. We'll just have to see what he's planning. At least he's taking us out to dinner."

So there we were, strolling in the church square, hot, but with a breeze. The flamboyant trees lining the boulevard could put anyone in a better mood even if you were feeling grumpy. I have to say that we must have been a good-looking trio. Papá walking straight as the soldier he was. Trim and groomed with a gray handlebar mustache and lemony cologne. His white suit perfect and his tie a little crooked as always. But his elegant ebony cane put him in absolute command. The General proudly strutted along with one of us on each arm, politely greeting strolling neighbors. Papá was doing it, creating the desired effect of the influential government official and caballero, accompanied by his two obedient, maiden daughters of the Republic. Oh brother!"

"Girls," he said as we began to eat our papaya piraguas (papaya snow-cones) sitting on a garden bench, "I took you out tonight to tell you of the great honor that is being bestowed on you: you are each going to be the first schoolteachers to open two brand new schools in the countryside. These are schools I built under that government development project I managed in the towns of Colombina and San Pedro. It took five years to construct real town squares with paved town roads and schoolhouses! Literacy, literacy, literacy for the campesinos (farmers)! And my daughters, the certified profesoras (teachers) will make this happen. We'll have opening ceremonies in each town, with speeches, parades, and music. It will all be fabuloso, niñas! Just fabulous, girls! During the school year you'll live in the towns, each with a nice family, like you did for the Census, and come home on weekends...."

When we finished our piraguas, we each took one of Papa's arms and walked home stunned, in total silence, the ache of our dictator's iron fist burning in our bellies. Would our lives ever be our own?"

Rose
13
New York at Last
New York City, 1930s

After money and money, and months that turned into over a year, Goya and I received our permanent visas for moving to the United States. These were green cards saying we could live in the U.S. as official residents with prearranged employment. Goya was the one with the big job. I was the one with the dreams. His old business friend, Enrique, was doing well with the food markets he'd opened in Manhattan and the Bronx. The deal was that Enrique made Goya manager of all the stores, but really this was the job title to let him into the country. In fact, Goya was putting money into Enrique's business and had already given him most of it. My husband figured he already knew how to run small stores and that he would be just as successful as in our country. We thought it was a perfect set-up.

Papá was not happy with my move. First of all, it meant I would now not be even a little under his control. Most important to him, it meant Goya's money would be invested elsewhere, and away from the generous donations he made to *Papá's* political party.

But the most unhappy ones were Patti and Nina. They cried and cried on finding out Goya and I were leaving—without them. Although I had in fact made four applications for U.S. residence, the only approval papers that came through were Goya's and my own.

But I had to go, even if it meant the girls were left temporarily with bossy *Papá,* alone in that big house. At this point, our three brothers were very much away from home and into their own lives. Victor still lived with the mistresses at the *Colegio Metodista* - they had basically become his mothers. Studying both theology and accounting at the University, Victor was becoming a fine young man. He visited *Papá* maybe twice a year; however, under the thin veil of their roles as father and son, Victor and his *Papá* were really strangers to each other.

Milo, who I always corresponded with, now had four of his own children. And, as the one and only schoolteacher and educated person in his town, he was taking on the role of humble, young elder among his townspeople. He never saw or spoke to *Papá.* As for Dio, he was lost. I mean really lost. When he ran away from the military school *Papá* enrolled him in, he completely disappeared. He was on the way to becoming one of the deep tragedies of our family.

On Puerto Rey's political front, a new president, Raúl Galante, was elected in 1933. An extremely large, round man with a booming voice, this president was wasting no time forbidding political activities unrelated to his own party. Our father was furious because it meant halting the works of the Party that he and his colleagues had formed with so much effort. *Papá's Partido Popular* (Popular Party) had run their own candidate on the same political ticket with Raúl Galante. This candidate lost badly, as did everyone else on the ballot. But what this meant to the new government, was that our father, General Bernardo Beltrán and his colleagues, were at best, outcompeted and reluctant supporters of the new administration; at worst, enemies of the new state.

In that year of 1933, those political affairs and how they would potentially affect our family were lost to my feverish preparations for a new life in the United States. And so, with many kisses and tears and promises to bring the girls to the U.S. as soon as possible, Goya and I left. I did not embrace my father when I gave him the respectful daughter's kiss of goodbye.

After fifteen days at sea, Goya and I were standing like two shivering children on Pier 42 of New York City's Hudson Harbor. We were in the middle of a wild crowd like we had never seen before. "*¿Dios mio, que es esto?*" (My God, what is this?) Fellow travelers who had disembarked from our ship, the *Vagabundo II*, were everywhere. Families in circles were kissing and hugging. Black men in red caps pushed long carts of luggage. And the noise—crying, calling out names, whistles shrieking, horns beeping from yellow taxis on the street. Would our, oh so helpful cousins, Zoraya and Nino, ever find us here? After three years of living in NYC, they were the experts on everything American. These cousins were our initial

U.S. contacts and help. Thank goodness! They had arranged an apartment for us in their own building at 160th Street and Riverside Drive.

On the pier, a cold push suddenly slammed into our backs. It was a big gust of freezing wind shoving everyone on the pier slightly to the left. W-w-welcome to New York! For me, it was the sign to pull out something absolutely fabulous from my carry-bag, a fluffy fox collar with dangling feet and two heads. The glass eyes were missing, but it was gorgeous anyway. For Goya, the icy moment signaled his tropical manhood to retract deep into his belly. The linen suit and Panama hat he had insisted on wearing did nothing to hide his Caribbean nakedness.

After collecting our luggage, we finally found our waiting cousins, who drove us to their apartment building in a fancy blue sedan. Zoraya talked and talked about the New York weather, safety, subways, where to shop, and a million other things we would have to learn. I listened, but I couldn't stop looking out the window at the giant *edificios* (buildings) and the people walking so fast. Naturally I tried to see what the women were wearing, and to tell you the truth, I thought that I fitted right in. I sat up a little straighter and as tired as I was, I began to smile. "This is going to be good," I said to myself.

But looking over at Goya, there he was, white as a ghost and trembling all over. His hat got lost in the wind and the vented tropical shoes he was wearing tore a little, so that his bunions were sticking out. "Oh my God, Fat

Feet, what's the matter with you?" I wanted to say. "We're in New York. Pull yourself together!"

It was night by the time we arrived at Zoraya and Nino's building—and our new home. It was at the end of a very long downhill street stacked on both sides with buildings and more buildings. The front entrance of 1225 Riverside Drive was unlike anything I'd ever seen before. Marble steps led to big, black iron doors with brass handles. On each side of the steps were tall iron lamps standing on round lion heads, and at the top, enormous bulbs that lit up the entrance like daytime. With suitcases, and nerves and nonstop chatter from Zoraya, we fell into the lobby. All we saw in front of us was a shiny green door with black buttons on the right side. Zoraya pressed the top button. Above the green door was a row of numbers from one to eight that were lighting up one by one. Inside the door was definitely some kind of machine that made noise. "Oh, *un elevador* (an elevator)!"

All of a sudden, the green door opened and a big woman who looked like she had muscles under her coat, almost crashed into us as we held the door open for her. Zoraya sang, "*Meellie, Meellie*, you are perfect in time to meet my cousin Rose. We just got them at the boat from Puerto Rey."

"*Rooose*, you gorgeous *goil*," said Millie Brecher. "You are stunning. And from who did you get that suit, darling?"

"I made it," I said.

"Really, you made it darling? So, they know peplum jackets in that, that Puerto place, where you're from?"

"*Si, como no*. I mean *jes,* we have all the fashions that we copy from America."

"And I am a tailor," said Millie. "You see these coats on hangars I'm carrying? A late delivery. We'll talk, I have to go. But wait, who is the frozen man?"

"Rose's husband," said Zoraya, as she looked over to the pale and trembling Goya.

Our furnished fifth-floor apartment had a living room with big, tall windows, one bedroom, and a kitchen with a gas stove you could light with matches. No wooden branches to burn, like in my country. The living room was pleasant looking but very cold because the wind came in through the window edges. We were right above Riverside Park and the grey Hudson River was just below it.

Goya wondered whether the cold was chasing him. He didn't like being in that parlor, so we spent a lot of time in the kitchen, making coffee and plans. We were basically okay with the apartment. It was a sublet for a year. And there was enough money, we hoped, until Goya's business plans got going and I got a job.

But, by the end of the second week, we discovered that something was very wrong. Goya had traveled by subway five times – getting lost every time – to meet his partner Enrique, at a place in the Bronx. Enrique never showed up. The man called at night to make his excuses but continued to be absent from every meeting. Goya was beginning to suspect that he had been cheated. My husband's state was terrible. He was nervous, wouldn't eat, and one time I thought I heard him crying in the bathroom. I felt terrible for him and, honestly, guilty, because if it wasn't for me, we wouldn't even be here. I was the one who for years kept my eye on coming to New York - dreaming, learning English, talking constantly about the States. I knew very well that my talk was my threat to my husband. I was going to leave Puerto Rey, no doubt about that. And he knew it. He came with me to avoid losing me, and he might have lost a fortune in the process. *Dios mío,* my God, what was going to happen to us?

I have to confess that I couldn't stand Goya being in the apartment: his mood, my guilt, our tension with each other. On the days he was out chasing his partner or getting people to help him find a solution, I breathed a little and cleared my head. The best part was that Millie and Zoraya would come over. Millie Brecher and I loved each other instantly. Her big smiling face didn't tell you that she had buried her husband in transit to America. As Jews trying to leave Poland, they were beaten at the train station by the police on the day of their departure; and her Herman was hurt very badly.

"Darling," said Millie. "There are so many of us here now, in this very building, even. My country will not be a possible place for us to live anymore. And the worst is still coming."

In my new American kitchen, we were all starting new lives, and I had to think hard about how I would go about doing that. I knew how to keep business books, I knew how to make women's clothes, and I had a good eye for styles. So these were the jobs that I was going to look for. I felt in a big rush to do this because by two months after our arrival, it was obvious that Goya had really been swindled.

My husband was in a terrible state now, smoking and smoking and pacing the apartment. He scared me because sometimes I heard him say to himself, "This is hell, a freezing hell... We're leaving, we have to leave..." Then he would run out of the apartment and walk for hours. What I was afraid of was that he would come back and say, "Rosa, start packing, we're going home – there is nothing for us here– this is a big mistake."

But I was staying no matter what. I desperately needed a job, not only for money but to put an official stamp on my decision to make my life here. To tell you the truth, apart from my husband's bad luck, I had a secret feeling of positivity around me, like I was moving on a wave, about to find my sunny beach soon. Goya was in such a different place. You could see it. You could feel it. His was a wave of cold and darkness.

The warm connection between Millie and I grew quickly. It was like we were destined to be close friends. Her tailoring orders were big now, so she needed a second person to complete the jobs. And here I was. Not as professional as Millie, but knowing enough from what my godmother Lola taught me, to do all the finishing. And I got better every day. We worked mostly in the kitchen, but when the weather was warmer, we made a little shop in my living room where the light was bright and sunny. Oh, those lady neighbors loved to be measured and fitted in my parlor with the little *cafecitos* we offered them. The windows still leaked, but the great business plans we were making kept our engines moving. When my cousin Zoraya, without her husband Nino knowing, gave Millie and me 300 dollars to buy two brand new Singer sewing machines, a worktable, and all the needles, pins, thread, snaps, scissors and measuring tapes a tailoring shop could need—we knew we were officially in business!

After six months of working together day and night, we had enough money to pay ourselves small salaries and pay Zoraya back her gift. I tracked our money, being very careful to keep our bookkeeping private and separate from my household money. Goya's business luck had not changed, nor had his wild desire to seek revenge on his partner, whom he was still hunting down instead of looking for another job.

As for our tailoring, when two back-to-back orders came in for dressing bridal parties, Millie and I knew we were official. Working one hundred hours a day, we were over the moon! The newest crazy dream was to open a ladies' fine dress shop on upper Broadway, decorated with carpet and wallpaper. This conversation was for our ears only.

I wish I could say that Goya's losing his investment was the only terrible thing that happened to him that year. He and I were not happy together, and he felt like a stupid immigrant in a big city that was filled with only failure for him. I was obviously moving in my own direction. We no longer had any reason for intimacy of any type. The little we had together was now totally broken. However, in the middle of this hurricane, something even more unimaginable happened to my husband.

The word from home was not good. After only two years in office, the new presidency was instituting big reforms in every phase of Puerto Reyan life. All residents had to carry identification; private businesses were now under government supervision; and it was becoming clear that complaints about the state of affairs in the country were not encouraged. One Tuesday morning in our New York apartment, the doorbell rang with a telegram addressed to Goya, from his brother in Catalina. "Return home immediately," it said. "The Commerce Department has seized and closed your seven stores. You must report to court in three weeks. You are charged with illegal commercial activity and absentee management."

We were shocked. Goya had left a trusted manager in each of his business locations, with his brother overseeing. He dropped into the nearest chair, put his head in his hands and sobbed. "*Estoy ruinado.*" (I'm ruined.)

The following Monday, on a cold spring morning, Goya and I rode in silence in a taxi headed for Pier 42 on the Hudson. My husband had booked a one-way ticket home for one person on the *Vagabundo II*, the same ship that brought us to New York. We barely embraced for our goodbye. We knew the marriage was over.

Rose
14
Patriot of the Republic
Catalina, Puerto Rey, 1938

Cable Caribe/Western Union 7/Nov/1938
Papá ha fallecido. Venir imediatamente.
Papá has died. Come immediately.

On October 23, 1938, when he was eighty-two years and one day old, *Papá* asked Israel to help him dress in one of his linen suits, a white shirt, and a dark tie. The vest was an afterthought after feeling the morning chill. *Papá* wanted to take a picture. His shoes were polished as always, and he held his cane for the photo. It was important that his straw hat be visible at his side as if he were ready to take a walk. In the picture, if you look closely, you'll see that old *Papá* had even tried to wax his mustache. He didn't fuss much with his tie. Israel took the picture with *Papá* standing tall on the front porch, a slight smile on his face. *Papá* said, "Give this photo to Rosa when she comes." Then he asked to be undressed and put to bed. A lung infection. Our father, General Bernardo Beltrán, was dead fifteen days later.

Why did our parents both die of bursting chests that could no longer hold their beating hearts? I have never been able to understand that. Did our country do that to them? Did their struggle to make a better place finally take them? Why is it the same story with us Latins? *El Pueblo* (the people) elect a president. The president becomes a corrupt brute; the brute is taken by a coup; we put our hopes in a new regime; and it starts all over again. Nothing changes.

Anyway, I would never live in my country again. I knew my place now—it was the United States. So, with the news of *Papá's* death, I went back to Puerto Rey to do many things—bury my father, get my sisters Patti and Nina out of there and legally end my marriage with Goya. He and I had kept in touch by letter since his leaving me in New York four months earlier. Goya was charged with commercial negligence and the government repossessed most of his stores. I knew that he was now truly broken. I felt very badly for Goya, but I had to properly finish with the man so we could each go on with our own lives.

When I arrived at my father's house, Patti and Nina were waiting for me on the front porch, sitting on their rockers. They were wearing dark mourning clothes. When we ran toward each other and squeezed together hard, the familiar scent of our skin, hair and talcum, all mixed together to comfort our sadness. The girls looked pale and frightened. As much as they fought against the grip of *Papá's* iron fist, he was also the only thing holding their lives together. This was going to change.

The house was busy. It almost looked like past times when *Papá's* projects kept soldiers and messengers running in and out with dispatches. A group of elderly men in the parlor slowly made their way into *Papa's* study. Jacinto was there, General Beltrán's comrade from the time of the 1911 turmoil, and there was Lionel, *Papa's* colleague from the old Ministry. He smiled warmly as he hobbled over to me. I recognized so many of them. These were old soldiers from the early years of our nationhood, now coming to pay their last respects to the General. There was a gentleman in the group who was not familiar to me, but by the deference paid to him by the others, I guessed correctly that he was the President's official sent to acknowledge our father and arrange for a funeral befitting an early patriot of the nation.

As strange as this was, it made political sense. Remember that my father was never a Raúl Galante sympathizer. His party in fact ran a presidential candidate against him. But the old General was a fighter in his day, trying to overthrow an earlier dictatorship; and later, in the next administration, engineering the development of rural towns with roads, schools and town plazas. These patriotic acts were broadly known, and Galante would do best to acknowledge our father with some type of state gesture at the end of his life. But Big Galante, as he liked to be called, also never forgot a slight, and this too he acknowledged in the frightening period following our *Papá's* state funeral.

The family started to arrive at our home for the ceremonies. Lola, my godmother and my savior after

Mamá's death came in bustling with trays of coffees for everyone. Then there was our *Tía* Teresa, *Papá's* maiden sister, whose clenched jaw and severe bun spoke of the usual state of her heart. Just as Lola could lighten a room with her lovely spirit, so could *Tía* sour the cream in anyone's coffee. The funeral was the following day, and we worried that none of the brothers had arrived yet. Finally, around nine p.m., after driving the bumpy roads from the countryside, Miss Laura arrived in her old car with the handsome, gentlemanly baby brother, Victor, at her side. We barely recognized this tall young man with a suit and bow tie, who was also carrying a Bible. A Bible? He was shy, and quiet and timidly put his hand out to me as if to formally shake it; but I pulled the boy toward me with all the strength of the big sister who long, long ago had tried to be his mother.

No one slept that night, listening for the sounds of our unburied father roaming through his earthly home. Around midnight I heard the front door open and quietly close. Someone was definitely in the house. I had to go and see. In the low light of the front hall was a very tall man in light-colored clothing. He removed his hat and said, "Rosa?"

"*Papá?*"

But my otherworldly moment was over when Patti, now standing behind me, turned on the full hall lights and we saw that it was our big brother Milo looking exactly like a young *Papá.* The same cocoa-colored face, tall, tall body and long, long arms.

"*Muchacho, donde has estado?* (Boy, where have you been?)" I said.

"*Pues, buscando a Dio por las calles, se ha totalmente desaparecido.* (I've been looking for Dio in the streets, he's totally disappeared.) We were going to meet by the harbor and come home together. He was afraid to come alone. But some of his old drinking boys told me that after a day of throwing back all the drink he could get his hands on, he disappeared."

We were all in the front hall now. No one spoke until *Tía* Teresa snapped, "Well, the Almighty knows where he is. Let's go to bed now. Tomorrow will be a long day."

General Bernardo Beltrán, *Papá,* age 82

We all awoke the next morning with cold stones in our stomachs. I didn't sleep at all, especially after hearing about our vagabond Dio. What was going to happen to him? So many worries. I cried all night for *Papá,* for my mess of a marriage, for Goya's ruin, for my innocent sisters. They were like babies in the woods after so many years of living under our *Papá*. Now they were my responsibility. What should I worry about first... what should I do first? *Mamá,* why aren't you here? Why do I have to always be in charge?

Everyone came to morning breakfast dressed in their funeral attire. The dark circles under their eyes told me they had not slept either. The girls were weepy, Miss Laura was stone-faced, and my little brother Victor looked like a teenage preacher, asking if he should read a section of the Bible to comfort us. What a group! I forced on my serious-strong-woman expression and raised my voice over the breakfast, *"Familia, alto. Hoy es el entierro de nuestro padre. Tenemos un mandado del Presidente Galante que el funeral será un acto de estado para un Patriota de la Nación."* (Family, listen. Today is our father's funeral. We have a statement from the Capital that our father's burial is going to be a state ceremony.)

But before I could tell them the order of the day's events, we heard a roar of noise outside the house. Wagon wheels came to a stop right at the front door. Horses clopped on the bricks, and men were shouting orders. We all ran at once to look and couldn't believe what we saw. Our father's mahogany coffin was neatly placed in the middle of a shiny open wagon and covered with a Puerto Reyan flag. The wagon was draped all around in black and purple taffeta. Sitting stiffly in the driver's seat was a soldier in uniform, firmly guiding two white horses fitted with military tack. Pulling up behind the wagon were four more horses, two Paso Finos and two red Sorrels. The President's military men rode the Pasos, while two quite elderly *compadres* (close friends) of our father were mounted on the Sorrels. Sitting as straight as they could manage in their Spanish saddles and high boots, they looked like *Papá* with their white mustaches and wrinkled faces. Their uniforms were, of course, from an earlier regime. I cried when I saw them, and I think they did too.

We turned to look at the very front of the procession where our Israel, dressed in one of his master's old dark suits, was positioning Capitán Jidalgo Rivera II, right in front of the funeral wagon. Cappy II, as we called him, was the son of *Papá's* old Paso Fino, who had taken him into fighting, into hiding, and into exile long ago when we were children. Cappy II was in full regalia with his silver-studded bridle and the country's coat of arms lying proudly on his breastplate. There was a purple sash under the enormous saddle—the saddle with the broad pommel and cantle that held a soldier firmly in his seat. But what touched us most were *Papá's* military boots, placed in the saddle stirrups backward, pointing away from the forward-moving horse: the sign of a fallen soldier.

One of the government's men then trotted briskly up to Israel, barking at him to leave the line—that he was the one ordered to lead the procession. "*Nunca* (never)," says the usually mute Israel. "This is my General's mount. Capitán and I will be the ones to lead our master to his resting place."

Israel planted his feet firmly on the ground, took control of Cappy's reigns on the left side, and stared straight ahead, prepared to lead the cortege at his signal. But just before the officer could begin to lash out, we all heard a rumble driving down the road—it was a flatbed truck, stopping and releasing four sweating soldiers with trumpets and drums. They knew their exact places right in front of the funeral wagon and behind the lead horse. Then Israel did the most daring thing we ever, ever saw him do in public. He raised his free arm, and firmly shouted, "Vamos, hombres," (Onward, men) at the top of his lungs. The band instantly started to play, all the horses pulled up, and *Papá's* funeral cortege was on its way.

Very like the day of our mother's burial, I don't remember everything. We, the children and the rest of the family, walked and walked with the cortege down the main avenue, in the hot sun. People watched, and some men saluted. Then the special part was marching the Patriot's wagon across the short *"Puente de los Duques"* with soldiers saluting on each side. This was the old wooden bridge – The Dukes' Bridge – built in colonial times, down by the harbor. I'm being sarcastic, but why would you want your dead body crossed over that thing? It was built in the 1500s to honor the Spaniard dukes who came to exploit and enslave the Indigenous Puerto Reyans! I don't understand this country at all…

By the time we got to the burial ground, we were almost dead ourselves. The heat, our blistered feet and the sickening smell of lilies on our father's coffin made the day feel like another one of *Papá's* awful, severe demands. I wasn't proud of feeling this way. May God forgive me. A car finally came to pick us up at the cemetery. And when we got home, each ran to their room—our grief burnt by the heat of the day.

To my surprise, I slept in my room for hours. I awoke with a *susto* (fright) when Patti gently shook my shoulder. I was on the bed in my mourning clothes, rumpled and sweaty and shocked that I'd slept like a dead person all afternoon. There was the buzz of guests downstairs who had come to pay their respects. Patti looked at me with her gentle smile. I had not really appreciated or talked to her since my return. But now as Patti sat lightly on the bed stroking my back, I noticed that she was changed—her face older, more set-in focus as she spoke. "It's time to get up now, *querida* (darling). I made excuses for you—but you've got to do the duty now."

"Of course, of course," I said, getting up with wrinkles in my taffeta. "I'll just wash and put some lipstick on."

Before I turned away, she looked at me again with her new face and said clearly. "Big sister, you've got two jobs to do while you're here. Get our visas so we can leave this country. I don't care how much of the money *Papá* left us we have to spend. We've been his prisoners here. Do you understand? And, and, you have to do the decent thing with that man, Goya. He's here asking for you. You have to finish with him. Get your divorce. Be done, and then the three of us, you, me and Nina can start new together in New York!"

I was stunned at the clarity of my little sister's words. She held my eyes in her two button-sized ones, and for a moment she was the mother.

Downstairs, old friends greeted me warmly. The parlor and porches were glowing with the oil lamps, lit tonight instead of the electric lights. *Papa's* old boys were in his study, drinking toasts to the General who had fallen for the last time. I spotted Goya in the corner of the living room, watching my movements. The most painful memory I have of him is his storming out of our apartment, damning both me and my insane idea of moving to America. I had ruined him, he said. Ruined him. He was thinner and even older looking now. Coming over to me shyly, he gave me an embrace of respect, without rancor, without passion. I was very sad and cried in front of him with shame. My God, what a mess! And to think our entire marriage fiasco, with its twists and turns and my clever planning, was started by the actions of the man who was now in a coffin. Goya and I agreed to meet in three days to start our legal break. I got scared when he said there would be some conditions.

There was so much to do, but the following days of receiving visitors were filled with plates and more plates of sweets and coffees and small shots of rum. Our pleasant smiles were set like stones, but our minds moved round and round about what the future would bring now.

On the last night of the mourning observance, my sisters cornered me in the kitchen, each taking one of my hands. "Rose, it's over now, *Papá* is gone. We've fulfilled our daughterly duties to care for him and comply with all the crazy projects he forced us into. We want our visas for the U.S. now—no matter what *Papá* may have done to block them!"

I promised them, "Yes."

How could I do all this? I ran out the back door, into the yard and beyond it. Our orchid jungle – was still there: colors dripping from everywhere, yellow lady slippers spilling out of a hole in the palm tree, hummingbirds burying their pointy beaks deep into their flower flesh. And beyond was the little barn, home to *Papa's* horse, and the now very, very old Tula, who used to be *Mamá's* pony. Those beauties, shiny and brushed, came over and stood very close to me. I cried for a long time, for no longer being my mother's child, for no longer wanting to live in my country. I didn't know whether I was crying for my *Papá* too.

Rose
15
Get Out
Catalina, Puerto Rey, 1938

Since my arrival for the funeral, our helpers had been loving and gracious as ever, especially my beloved Tita, who always seemed to understand my burdens after my mother died. She entered my room on the morning of the first free day without mourners in the house, with something clearly on her mind.

"Tita, what is it?"

"*Señorita* Rosa, I don't want to upset you more than you already are, but I have to tell you something that is happening here. We are all terrified. Three times, three different men have walked past our house in the evening, looking straight at whoever is sitting on the front porch, and makes the death sign across his throat. Your sisters have seen them twice, and last night another one came by doing the same thing when *Tía* Teresa was sneaking her smoke. Can you believe it—even while a house is in mourning! What does this mean, *Señorita*? Are we in danger?"

I let Tita say no more and believed that this story was an expression of her own grief for the General. Since her employment with us since the age of twelve, his authority had always made her feel safe. And that protection, real or imagined, was now gone.

Oh, that Tita has always been a little emotional, I told myself. But a dark sort of feeling began to move inside me. I tried to push it away, took a deep breath, and to distract myself, had some more coffee and a look at the newspaper to see what was going on. I turned as always to the social page first. *"Sra. Jacinta de Sullivan wins the St. Francis of Assisi orchid contest for the fourth time for her entry of the Dillomillus Orchid."* Nothing new there. She's married to that American millionaire, for goodness' sake. And look at this: *"Sonia Alicia Matón marries Miguel Ignacio Molina at high mass in the San Tomás Cathedral."* Oh no, we went to school together. Sonia hated Miguel since we were kids. The parents always wanted that match. Sonia has either lost her mind or gotten herself pregnant, poor girl.

On the front page of the newspaper, the upper left:

"President Galante, builds church and monumental plaza for the town of Belmonte. The monument is a tribute to our leader himself and the province of his birth…"

"What? Belmonte needs urban development, not glorifying statues to the President!"

Then, on the newspaper's upper right front page:

Pursuant to the Administration's goals for the economic progress of our island nation, the Congress initiates a new stage of requirements for its loyal citizens and business owners:

1. Merchants must submit a yearly accounting of their inventories and earnings.

2. Commercial enterprises yielding profits of 5,000 pesos or more will be audited by the Department of Commerce.

3. Private land holdings of fifty hectares or more are subject to potential use by the government for security and/or military purposes.

4. The sales of all real estate, private and commercial, will be reviewed by the Department of Commerce.

As cited by the new regulations of the Puerto Rey government, loyalty and obedience to all statutes is the honoring of the President, Himself and the new code of our Puerto Reyan nation.

What, what? What was this? It was a police state... I think that's what they call this. No wonder government guys have been crawling all over our cacao farm in La Loma since *Papá* died last week. They wouldn't dare do it with him alive. And the men making the death sign—were they real? Were they saying they could hurt us now that *Papá* was gone? My God, what do I do first, take care of the properties or get me and the girls out, out of here? Get us out of here, of course! I had to get dressed. I was moving like a machine now. No time for crying. I would do that later.

It wasn't hard to figure out why my two sisters' visa applications had not been considered. *Papá* simply paid off the immigration office clerk to keep their forms at the bottom of the stack. So, I would simply pay the clerk now to bring them to the front. This kind of thing was very straightforward in our dear country. However, the business with our farm property would have to wait for another time, until I understood the government's new laws. Everything was changing.

As for Goya, I didn't know what *conditions* he was talking about, to file for the divorce. I would see him the following night to settle it. All I knew was that nothing would stand in the way of we three sisters moving our lives together *out* of this country and *into* the U.S. And the boys, well, they seem to have made their choices. May God protect them.

PART II
Patti

Patti
16
It's Me, Patti
New York City Harbor, Hudson River, 1939

It's me, Patti. I'm finally moving to America. Nina and I, "the girls" as they still call us, are on a really large ship called the *Ponce*. We embarked in Puerto Rey on June 21, 1939, and we'll finally be in New York in two hours. *Dios mío* (my God), being on the ocean has been like taking a magic potion that's swept my mind. I'm much calmer now. We were terrified in the few months before leaving our country, because of the threats. Israel, as always, our protector, sat on the front porch day and night with his oldest son—rifles in their hands, until we left.

So, *I'm* going to talk now. Not Rose, not *Papá*. I'm going to continue telling our story—about the lives that we three girls, Rose, Nina and me, Patti , made in America. I told myself that as soon as I got to the U.S., it was going to be different for me. For the first time, I was going to think and say what *I* wanted. I practiced this because quietness is my real way. In this whole story so far, how often have you heard me speak? *Un poquitico,* very little, right? Here's what I think: if you're smiling and still and agree with everything people say on the outside, then they leave you alone. You can think and say whatever you want inside. And no one knows. Only when something very, very big is happening – like the time I punched the girl who was torturing Nina – do I explode.

Patti and Nina's ship to the United States, the *Ponce,* 1939

I love my people but in my own way. Some of them are gone now. When I lose one of them, I go to a place like the bottom of the ocean, where fish scream and no sound comes out. It's dark there, with a lot of dead things and I can scream too. Then, when I get tired of that, all I want to do is come up. To the top where the sun is, and I can make myself okay again. Water is a powerful thing that can pull me down. It scares me. I threw *Papá* into the ocean while I was on this ship. I won't think about him. I did this with my *Mamá* too, a very long time ago. Some of my *pensamientos* (thoughts) about her are so far down that I think they have totally disappeared.

Um, *pero,* (but), that's not totally true. I *can* travel to deep places, sometimes. Do you think I didn't miss my *Mami* after she died? You're crazy. Rosie kind of became our mother, but it wasn't the same. The best thing I remember about my real *Mami* is how much she loved me and how soft her skin was. I used to touch her face when she carried me. When I did that, she would laugh and kiss my hands. Then Rosa became our mother, and she never carried us. I guess that was good because Nina and I, only three and four, almost like twin baby girls, instantly became like big little girls when our mother died. That's when my quietness started. I needed to look hard at everything around me because everything changed after *Mamá* left us.

Remember, we went to that school with the mistresses? They were nice but I mostly hung on to Rosa's skirt all the time and never talked. Neither did Nina. Where was our *Papá*? I thought he was dead too, the thing they said about *Mamá.* I thought that meant he would never come back, I wasn't sure. We were in that school for a long, long time. The only thing that could make me laugh was my brother, Dio. He was the funny boy. Our big brother, Milo, started to look a lot like *Papá* around then, and I liked that. He was another quiet one, like me and didn't smile too much, but you felt his heart when he looked at you. That was totally different from our father. I could never feel my *Papá*.

There's a baby story about me that our family tells, when they're in the mood at the *sobremesa* after dinner. That's the name we give to the conversation people have at the table when everyone is finished eating and having coffee. These *cuentos* (stories) almost always begin with the story of us brothers and sisters standing around the big mahogany bed where our mother died. *Mamá* was still holding baby Victor in her arms. Milo, Dio, Nina, and Rose were all standing around the bed; Rose was carrying me. We didn't move. We saw everything: how our mother's sad blue eyes looked at each and every one of us, over and over again. Like she was talking to us.

"*Mi dulce* (my sweet one)", she said to me. I don't know what she said to the others. The baby started to cry very low, almost like a kitty sound. We all watched with big eyes. It was hot in the room, and I remember I could see our reflections in the shiny mirrors that hung all around our *Mamá's* beautiful bedroom. Although I don't remember this part, my family says I suddenly yelled, "It stinks like poo in here!" I guess I smelled the baby's dirty diaper. The boys tried not to giggle. And I remember Rosie softly saying to me, "*Shhhh mi niña.*" Do you know, that after that moment, Rosie never held me again? Because our mother died *en ese mismo minuto* (in that very minute). She turned her face to the wall, closed her eyes, and let go of baby Victor. Then Rose, who was carrying me, put me down, took that baby prince into her arms, and carried him forever. Yes. It's true, forever... Hm, who wants Rose to hold you, anyway?

Something happened to me at the Mistress's school. I think that's why I was so sad there. I'm very, very scared of cats. They're bad things. Nina and I were the youngest little girls at the school, so when we weren't in the nursery room, we spent a lot of time in the kitchen with the cooks taking care of us. The meats were always roasted outside on a *brasero*—a grill that is low down, close to the ground. You can believe we stayed away from there because it was very hot, from the morning until after we ate dinner at night. I was playing outside collecting sticks when the ugly grey cat who ate the *ardillas* (squirrels) in the garden started to walk toward me. I stepped back and back, not taking my eyes off that scary furry ball, when *ayyyy,* I crashed right up against the burning *brasero.* "*Mami, Mami, Mami.*" I smelled the back of my leg cooking.

People in the kitchen came, lifted me up and took me running to Mrs. Wimble, the mistress who was the nurse. After giving me medicine that made me sleepy, she laid me on my stomach, then put ice all around my leg. I didn't know if I was freezing or burning. When I finally woke up, it was night and Mrs. Wimble, seated in a big chair, was holding me against her little bosom. Talking to me in her funny Spanish, she smiled and said, "*Mi niña, estás bien.*" (You're okay, little girl). My leg was so big because it was wrapped in coldness and pillows, and she fixed it so the cooked part wasn't touching anything. I think I got very sick with a fever, but *Mamá* was *muerta* (dead) and *Papá* was lost. I don't remember where Rose was. No, I can't think about these things. I have to throw them back into the ocean.

Then, I finally see it. "Look, Nina, it's New York, the skyscrapers!"

We're both hanging onto the ship's rail together with the other passengers. The *Ponce* is finally floating into the New York Harbor. Here we are, wearing almost the same black dresses with flowers all over them, like twin girls – very chic – and straw hats with black ribbons around the big brims.

"We passed the Statue of Liberty about an hour ago. Why are we waiting to pull into the pier? I know Rose is there, she's there waiting for us. I can see some small boats around us like they're guiding our ship in. I can't stop moving my feet, my heart is jumping. This is our moment!"

Nina and I left Puerto Rey, together of course, a few months after the death of our father. Rose was pushed by her fear for our safety, and using her bossy and probably sneaky ways, finally got our visas to leave the country. Oh, and she got her official divorce from Goya, too. She was free now. We, girls, could never live in our country again with the terrifying threats we got after *Papá's* funeral. The boys stayed, but I'll get to that later.

I was holding on tight to the ship's rail. I just couldn't keep still. The ship was slowly, slowly getting closer to the pier. I don't think I've ever felt so happy, ¡*Que alegría*! Nina just whispered saying, "*Ay Dios*, oh God," with that stone face of hers. I said, "*Hermanita* (little sister), I want you and everybody to know it's going to be different with me from now on. In fact, I don't want to be called Petra ever, ever again. She's gone. I'm Patti, of the United States. That's it. I'm going to run my own life—I know what I want: to become an American citizen. To marry a beautiful man who will love me. And to be the mother of a wonderful child—hopefully a girl. But whatever God gives me is okay." Nina stood at the rail, saying nothing.

On the ship, Nina was definitely not the most chatty companion. But I really pushed her. It was only the two of us out in the ocean and we were on our way to changing our lives so completely.

"What do you want in New York, Nina? What do you think? I'm putting the past behind me. Are you?" She mumbled some *yes* kind of answers, but mainly, Nina read her books and tried to stay out of the sun on the deck. But I have to say she always looked beautiful—and so did I, I think. We got to wear the dresses we had been sewing and saving for years for our move. My sister, though, was fairer skinned, closer to our mother's ivory tone, and I always thought she looked more special. Would they notice this in the U.S.? I saw that Nina's green card visa said, "Race: white," and mine said, "Race: India." That means what they also call "Indigenous." I had the same skin tone as Rose. I wondered what her "Race" said.

My way to pass the time on the ship was walking round and round the sunny deck and making shy English conversations with the other travelers. We were in the middle deck, not rich, but also not poor. Mostly, Nina and I kept to ourselves; after all, we were two young ladies traveling alone, with no arrangements made by parents to be chaperoned on the ship. You could say that we were totally orphan girls now.

I had lots of time to think, like I told you—confusing things, sad things. "*Mami*" I heard inside my head sometimes. And as for *Papá*, "that old man, keeping us like prisoners to take care of him. Holding back our visas! *Viejo sin verguenza* (shameless old man). I'm making you disappear. You are dead forever." And when I threw him down into the Atlantic Ocean from the deck of the ship, I was "okay." And that became my best American phrase.

After days of anticipation and doing some of the most serious thinking I had ever done about my life, we finally docked into New York Harbor. As Nina and I timidly came down the ship's steps, almost losing our balance on new high heels, we saw our Rose right there on the pier's edge. Her red coat and hat made sure we noticed her right away. But the kissing and hugging would have to wait for a long hour until the U.S. Customs processed our papers after disembarking from the ship.

Nina and Patti's arrival in America from Puerto Rey, 1939

Finally, we three laughing sisters packed ourselves into a big, yellow taxi with all of our luggage and boxes, and took a very bumpy ride along the West Side Highway to Rose's house. After a half-hour ride, our big sister announced in English, "We're home!"

As we fell out of the cab with all our things, I realized that I was in front of the tallest apartment building I had ever seen. Slowly, we began to enter the building's lobby, where there was a big green door to our right that said ELEVATOR, on the front. I knew from Rose about these motor boxes that took you up and down. We repacked our suitcases and ourselves into the motor thing and our big sister pressed the number six button. We three went up, with very funny noises, to the sixth floor. By this time, we were sick and tired of all our luggage and just left it outside the sixth-floor elevator door as we followed Rose who was running down the hallway toward her apartment, 6B. She opened the door – we were behind her – and there inside, was a crowd of people yelling "Welcome, welcome, *bien venidas.*" They were Rose's friends, the Americans.

A short, stocky woman who was laughing and pushing herself in front of everybody with her big chest, threw her arms around me and said, "I'm Millie, Millie Brecher, Rose's best friend, business partner, and so many other things—you *goils* are gorgeous, gorgeous. I'm from Brooklyn, once from Poland, but I live in the building now."

Nina tried to smile but couldn't cover the look of shock as everyone came over to hug us, hug her. She hated being touched.

There was Atta, a tall, big German woman with a beautiful pink and perspiring face, who extended her hand formally, saying, "How do you do? I'm Mrs. Golda Levine, but call me Atta. I live next door in 6A."

Then, there was a couple standing together—Sonia and Hugo. They looked like movie stars. Sonia must be the Miss Puerto Rico (1933) Rose told me about who lived two floors up. I'd never seen such big, red lips in my life.

And there was another couple, Zoraya and Nino, cousins I recognized from Puerto Rey who are brand new citizens in the U.S. now.

Suddenly we turned toward a loud voice coming from Nancy Russo—a tiny Sicilian woman with a big, big laugh and a very short, very black pixie haircut. She said to me, "Oh Patti, I can tell, we're *gonna* be real good friends."

Rose then directed our attention to a very good-looking gentleman, *caballero*, coming slowly toward us. He bent slightly at the waist as he took our hands. "*Yo soy Jorge Gavilán de Caracas. A sus ordenes.*" (I'm Jorge Gavilán from Caracas, at your service.) "*Umm, guapísimo,*" (super handsome) I said to myself. Out of the corner of my eye, I saw Rose blush.

I cannot tell you the joy, the music, the food, that filled that apartment on the day of our arrival. We were here now. Our Rosie had done it, and even though she wasn't the sweetest baby *Mami*, she sure could make things work in the big world. And I wanted some of that too. *Moverme, desempeñarme, y hacer mi vida.* (To move myself, to act, and make my own life.)

Finally, bed. But as exhausted as my body was, I was too excited to sleep. "Nina, Nina, Nina Maria. Are you awake? Didn't we have a great time? Weren't those beautiful people? They're going to be our new friends."

I kept trying to wake Nina, but she was too far gone into her snores. So, I got out of bed and tiptoed into the dark hallway. There was a light coming from the kitchen at the far end of the apartment. I had to cross the living room to get there and noticed for the first time since I arrived, that there was a thick, green carpet and the wall at the end of the room was covered from floor to ceiling with a mirror. Wow! This was beautiful. So, this was what Rose meant by "decorating the apartment like Americans."

I quietly called out, "Rosa, Rosie." As soon as she saw me, she smiled in a great big way and told me to sit down and have a cup of strong coffee with her—the best way to fall asleep. I saw that her face was happy, but her eyes were red and saying something else.

"What's wrong, big sister?"

"Have your coffee first," she said. Hoping to lighten her mood, I teased her about the handsome *caballero* from Caracas. "Yes, yes, stop it, so we like each other," she said with a giggle. "But that's not what I want to tell you. I'm pregnant, Patti, and it's Goya's baby."

She started to cry, and I put my arm around her.

"I'm so ashamed of myself. When I was back in Catalina for *Papa's* funeral, and arranging for the divorce and your visas, and everything for the entire world, Goya had the nerve to say he would give me a divorce if I had, you know, relations with him one last time, as his wife. I didn't know whether to feel furious with that *sin verguenza* (shameless stinker) or sorry for him because he lost everything in the U.S., because of me. So, I did it, and now I have his baby in me. I don't want a baby now, Patti. I thought I would never have children of my own after what happened in our fam... Oh, never mind! I just can't be a mother now when everything else is starting in my life. I love it here. And now it's perfect with you two girls here. I've got so many plans. Millie and I are about to lease a ladies' dress shop right around the corner on Broadway. Can you imagine? A real business. And then I'll open another and another."

For almost the first time, I saw everything Rose wanted for herself and her terror at being blocked again like she was before: by our country, our family, our father and the endless proper obligations she was forced to perform ever since she was made the big-sister-mother. I tell her that night that I would help her do whatever she wanted, whatever she needed.

In promising myself to Rose as the keeper of her secret, I grew that night, feeling for the first time that we were partners in making a new life. We held each other for a long time as we said goodnight. We were both sleepy now after those cups of coffee—American coffee.

"Oh, one more thing," my big sister said, as each of us turned in the hallway toward our rooms. "Do not tell Nina, not until I figure out what to do."

"Don't worry, Rosie," I giggled. "I don't know if she even knows how babies are made."

"*Buenas noches,*" we said together.

Patti
17
Working
New York City, 1939

Our new days in our new country became a happy routine very quickly. We worked hard during the day, studied English at night and made our dreams for the future. Rose had some friends who helped Nina get interviews with New York companies needing multilingual secretaries. Nina's strange and perfect knowledge of English, French and Italian, in addition to Spanish, put her in excellent chance of getting a very, very good job.

But Nina was not hired by any of the companies who met with her. And we heard why. Her skills were apparently excellent, but no one liked her personality. She didn't smile or make small talk at an interview; was just serious and stern, simply listing her qualifications. Can you imagine? So, Rose and I gave her some lessons on being a little bit charming, *simpática*, and showed her how to smile when she answered a question. Then guess what? She got the very next job she interviewed for. We were so proud of her! She looked like an elegant professional lady every morning as she left the house for work; tall, slim, and dressed in beautiful stylish clothing that Rose tailored for her. But there wasn't a single morning that we didn't say, "Smile, girl." To tell you the truth, we worried about our little sister. We knew that her innocent face could not cover the dark shadow that seemed to live inside her. Neither Rose nor I would ever admit it openly, but we knew there was something happening with our girl.

I was happy with everything. My job was working in Rose and Millie's new store. I learned something new every day. I loved keeping track of the inventory as bolts of fabric, patterns and new machines came in. I was good at it. I dressed the mannequins in the window with new styles made in our shop. There were two more seamstresses at the store now, in addition to Rose and Millie. The big orders for weddings were really coming in now. Some days I took the D train down to the fabric and sewing district on Seventh Avenue. I always had a specific job—to find the perfect buttons for a suit or the exact color of seam-binding for a strapless dress.

Nedick's on 48th and 7th avenue was my favorite place for lunch. It was a hot dog on a toasted bun with mustard and sauerkraut and a cold, cold orange soda with bits of orange in it. I don't want you to think that I went to the same place for lunch because I didn't know how to handle myself. I just loved hot dogs – *perros calientes, as they say* – a really American thing.

My English got better and better, except for the accent. But my girlfriend, Fannie, said it was glamorous. Anyway, we told these funny jokes, laughing at ourselves as immigrants. "A new *imigrante* goes to the same luncheonette every day. He doesn't speak any English so he asks a friend how to order apple pie and coffee. He learns how to say this very, very well: *applepieantcoffee, applepieantcoffee*. So, he orders this every day, every day. He gets sick of it and asks the friend to teach him how to order another dish. So, the *imigrante* learns how to ask for ham and eggs. *Hamneggs,* he practices, *hamneggs*. He goes to the diner and asks the waiter for *hamneggs*. The waiter smiles and says, "Sure mister. Want those eggs sunny-side up or sunny-side over? The *imigrante* answers: *applepieantcoffee*. Ha ha ha ha ha ha!

No matter how tired I was from work during the day, I loved going to our English night classes. A quick dinner and we were ready. Nina and I took the Broadway bus from our neighborhood up to George Washington High School in Inwood, three nights a week. During the day, the school was full of teenagers, but at night when we were there, it was full of people just like us. They were from everywhere. Mr. Cho was from Hong Kong, waiting for his sweetheart to arrive; and Elizabeth, a smiling blond girl, was from Austria. She became my best friend. Nina liked her too, but she had such a hard time joking around and chatting about things. Still, we always included her in our weekend plans to the big movie theaters downtown. There was the *Roxy* and *Radio City Music Hall* that always had live dancing shows with fifty girls, the *Rockettes*, all kicking perfectly in a row. And their costumes, wow! I loved this—my new life. So far, the past... my lost people… were staying deep down in the water where I put them.

Rose was running like an express train. She was unstoppable: make more money, get a new store, grow the business, and yes, see her *caballero*, Jorge, as much as possible. They were really in love now. Jorge was absolutely crazy about her. I was so happy for her—she really deserved this man's love.

Patti and Rose, the New Americans, 1941

Patti
18
Love
New York City, 1940

We three sisters were now like a knot tied tightly together—for better or worse. Nina and I filled Rose's apartment and life with chatter, more chatter, laughing and sometimes, yes, arguing. But we loved it all. Rose finally got us to my American dream place, and we would never separate again. I knew that Rosie felt relief when Goya left her and went back to Puerto Rey, but I also knew how lonely she had been by herself in this foreign city. My big sister made everyone believe she was fearless in her first years here. She just opened her mouth and some kind of English came out of it. All she knew was that people answered her, so she kept on going. Her secret as always was to look stunning in her beautiful suit (the same blue one for two years!) and fox shawl. (By this time, she had replaced its missing eyes with two tiny marbles—passable!)

About eight months after our arrival, on a Sunday afternoon in January 1940, Nina and I were getting ready to go to a downtown tea dance with some other girls. Live orchestras played in dance halls on the weekends—the perfect place for ladies and gentlemen to meet in the afternoon moonlight.

"Nina, so what are you wearing? I'm wearing my new blue taffeta with the ruffled collar."

"I'm not going."

"What? They're having a tango orchestra at the *Roseland Ballroom* this Sunday. Tango, do you hear me, tango! We've been practicing, *muchacha,* (girl) remember?" I pulled my pain-in-the-neck sister off the bed and started to dance with her. "Just follow the gentleman, long steps, kick your leg up in the back sometimes, look like you're surrendering to him, half close your eyes. Not in real life, of course."

We were laughing like crazy—I was the only one who could do that to her. Make her laugh, make her do things with me. But not always. I knew sometimes that she played with me in actions but not in spirit. At least we were together. But I wondered, would it always be my job to put life into her? This worried me.

Dressed up and looking our best, we met our friends, Elizabeth and Fanny, at the 168th Street subway station on Broadway. This was the big subway stop at the *Columbia Presbyterian Hospital*. The Eighth Avenue train was perfect for getting to *Roseland*—only three blocks of walking from the subway in our high dancing shoes.

Let me tell you that as soon as we paid our tickets, checked our coats, and went inside the dance hall, something happened to me. The round chandelier globes made a pinkish light around the room, and everyone,

everyone looked... I don't know, beautiful. So many *guápos,* handsome Latin men here in fine suits. Real *caballeros*—at least those were the ones I was looking at. And the girls, with beautiful hair that moved around when they danced. Mine didn't do that because I had a bob, but I knew how to sway my dress so it twirled when I danced. I practiced at home.

And the music! It's was *una fantasia* (a fantasy). No matter how loud or soft or perfectly tuned your radio was, nothing sounded like real live music. No matter what they played, swing or Latin boleros, I'm a little shy to say this, but a feeling came up inside me, in my stomach, that made me... I don't know... excited. Groups of girls like us were sitting at little tables with a drink and doing several things at once: sitting up elegantly so our bosoms popped up, looking pretty, and moving a little bit to the music to show that we wanted to dance. Then carefully, very, very carefully, we began to look at every single man who was dancing, at a table, or standing around the dance floor—of course, doing the same thing we were. Fanny and Elizabeth were so much better at this than I was. It wasn't my natural way. I got nervous when I looked at someone and he looked at me back. Oh God, what were you supposed to do? I didn't know. I didn't want to look *fresca* (fresh) by smiling. So, I turned my eyes toward the band, or the girls, or Nina who was usually reading the menu or the label on a wine bottle! This was terrifying, but I loved it!

After playing two gorgeous *paso dobles* (a two-step ballroom dance done to Latin rhythms), the band leader made an announcement about the tangoes in the next set. They were going to play a few selections by Carlos Gardel—probably the most famous tango singer in the world. As I was listening to this, I noticed a quite tall *caballero* making his way straight to our table and smiling a little at me—like in a shy way. As he crossed the dance floor, he removed his glasses and put them in the breast pocket of his navy suit. It was like slow motion. I looked directly back at him without even blinking, and by the time he got to my table and asked me to dance, I had already put down my drink and uncrossed my legs, ready to take his hand, when he softly asked, "*¿Señorita, me permite pedirle un baile?*" (Señorita, would you permit me to ask for a dance?) Before even answering, I took his arm. I didn't turn around to look at my girls or the band. I just went with him.

He was a man of few words. I thought he was Spaniard. He said he was Cuban. I saw him as a businessman. He said he worked in a restaurant. But this gentleman, his name was Gabriel Acosta, told me everything about himself in his dance. Leading me with clear gestures, he created all the spaces I needed to be beautiful on the dance floor, opening the windows for my turns, waiting the extra beat for my back-swings – they call those *ganchos* – and holding me just close enough to graze my cheek. We danced for what felt like a heavenly hour, until the tangoes were finished and the orchestra began the low moans of the *boleros*.

We understood each other's movements by this time—our starts, our breaks, our body rhythms to the music. We fit so well. I was afraid to realize that I wanted nothing more than to relax into this man. And I did, and he smiled. But at the end of the first *bolero*, perspired and flushed and other things too, we stopped.

"Let's drink something," he said, and we sat at the bar. There I could really see his face and physique instead of feeling him so pleasantly against me. He was fair, with very dark straight hair that was slicked back the way men wear it these days. His white shirt and tie knot were perfect, as were his fine black shoes. There was a quietness in Gabriel's way of being, and he told me that he was better at dancing than talking. But he managed to tell me that he was a single man living on the west side of New York. All he had done in the three years since arriving from Havana was work seven days a week.

"Why so much, aren't you killing yourself?"

"I'm trying to save money, that's all I want to do—and I'm almost there. In six months, I'll have enough to be my friend Johnnie's equal partner—we're buying a restaurant, a luncheonette in Perth Amboy, New Jersey. You know, just across the George Washington Bridge. I'll be an owner, that's what I've always wanted since I was *un niño*, a kid. And then who knows what more the future will bring?"

Gabriel asked me about my family and what I did in New York. I told him about us, the sisters, and how we were each creating new lives in the United States. Before I could even finish my story, he interrupted me to ask if I would meet him here at the *Roseland*, the following Sunday. His fair complexion turned pink as he asked.

Like a true gentleman, Gabriel took me back to my table where all the girls were waiting, dying to know who this man was. I introduced him all around to the wide-eyed girls, loving the way he shook each one's hand. And then he turned to me, and with a little bow he took my hand, and squeezing it, said, *"Encantado, Patti. Hasta el próximo domingo."* (Enchanted, Patti, until next Sunday.) And he disappeared into the crowd of dancing people.

The ride back uptown on the subway was full of wild noise. Between the rumble of the train and the girls all talking and asking me questions at once, I felt as if I was speeding down a tunnel toward places I had never been before.

"Who is this man?"

"Where does he live?"

"Does he have a job? Forget about anybody who doesn't have job! He's a real looker, shy though."

And Nina adds, "What if he's a Cuban assassin?"

The other girls laughed and laughed, but I know she wasn't kidding.

I couldn't wait to get home and tell Rose about our night. But as we came in the apartment door, Rose was laughing and dancing around the living room with Jorge.

"We're engaged, we're engaged," Rose yelled as soon as she heard us come in. "*Este señor,* this gentleman took me totally by surprise today. Can you believe we had a date to walk in Riverside Park today? Jorge made a whole picnic for us, with a blanket and chairs and everything. Then he asked me to marry him. Look at this ruby ring."

I couldn't believe this day! Gabriel and then, Jorge? Was there a full lady moon out there tonight sending us beautiful men?

"What a day, what a day," I said as I laughed and screamed and hugged everyone. I don't think I'd ever seen Rosie so happy. I liked how Rose was with Jorge, calmer, not so bossy. I'm not saying she was lesser—just that when Jorge was around, she was quiet-strong, instead of noisy-strong to show everybody. This was good. I loved Jorge for Rose. They fit together.

As we giggled and toasted with champagne, I realized that Nina had not crossed my mind for a while. Oh, she was there too saying all the right things, but I noticed her slight stiffness, her forced smile. When I asked, "Nina, aren't you happy for our big sister?"

She said, "of course," with lowered eyes, and in one swift motion, left the living room saying she needed to work the next day. But having a sharp ear for the tones of her voice, I heard her grumbling all the way down the hall to the bedroom.

I don't think I slept even for one minute that night. Could it be? Could it be that like Rose I could have someone who belonged only to me? It wasn't that I already loved Gabriel. That's silly—just that meeting him and seeing Rose and Jorge put the big idea in my mind, about love. So, what do I do now? I waited for the first drop of daylight to color the sky and got myself out of bed to make coffee. Enough of this crazy thinking, I had to go to work. But who was at the kitchen table wide awake, drinking her *café con leche* (coffee with milk)? Rose, of course.

She said, "*Patti mi vida, como te amaneces*? (Patti my darling, how are you this morning?) Last night was something, wasn't it? And, what happened at the dance yesterday with you girls? You came in all excited and I didn't hear anything from you."

I started giggling and blushing when she said this and spit out, "I met a gentleman there named Ga… Gabriel" I couldn't get it out, I couldn't stop laughing.

"Patti, *muchacha,* girl, look at you, look at you," said Rose, "¡*Estás enamorada*! You're in love!

"No, I'm not," I giggle. But I could feel myself getting red. I told my big sister all about this man and we made a plan. If I really liked Gabriel at *Roseland* next weekend, if I really judged him to be a gentleman, and he asked me out, and if I wanted to go—then, I could say yes. But he had to pick me up at home so he could meet my family. I felt excited to the moon when Rose said this! I was relieved too, because I didn't know how you did "dates" in New York, or really, anywhere. Back home in Catalina when we were with *Papá*, the only dates we had with young men were playing checkers on the front porch or going to little dances accompanied by a *chaperona*—

usually my *Tía* Teresa. It was awful. That all seemed like a hundred years ago.

We heard Nina coming down the hall toward the kitchen. "Good morning, girls," she said. "Why are you laughing before breakfast?"

Rose and I looked at each other and couldn't help giggling.

"Nina, what's wrong with you? It's 6:30 in the morning and you're already a sourpuss."

"I just can't stand all this, this excitement," she said. "Let me know when you've left the kitchen, and I'll come to make my own coffee." And she ran back into her bedroom.

Ay yay yay. Although we were both a little surprised at Nina, this didn't spoil our moment: Rose and I were in love!

Patti
19
The Dictators' Children
New York City, 1940

Every once in a while, when we couldn't sleep, when we were worried, when ghosts from our past demanded to be heard, when letters from our brothers tore at our hearts—Rose, Nina and I sat in the kitchen together, talking late into the night.

Over all the excitement of my first years in New York, I tried to think as little as possible about life in my country. I felt badly about this, but I didn't think there was enough room in my new mind to think about my old life. But the ghosts buried in my ocean – *Mamá, Papá*, and the young children we were with such tender hearts – sometimes came to life in our night kitchen.

We would speak the real family truths. When we were young, *Papá* considered us children, little humans to be molded into upstanding adults. Our feelings about any of his decisions for us were of no importance to him. Now on our own in New York, we understood that *Papá* neither loved nor hated us. We were simply the responsibilities left to him upon the death of our mother. This gave him permission, the right to do what he wanted with us, under the idea of fulfilling his duty: Put us into the boarding school; pull us out of the boarding school; disown his big boy Milo for leaving law school; reject Dio for being a troubled adolescent. And Rose, his eldest daughter? What he did to her hardened her heart. After she mothered all of us little ones, *Papá sold* her to an old man. I say *sold* because this is the secret word Rose used for the arranged marriage to Manuel Goya, *Papá's* important political benefactor.

As for Nina and myself, the youngest sisters, our father's harshness terrified us, such that we suffered from a weakness of will until we came to America. And finally, I will say the very, very forbidden, what all of us believed was true: *Papá* gave away our baby brother Victor. Yes, gave away, because deep down inside, he believed the baby had caused his beloved Estrella's death.

I know we got a little *dramáticas* (dramatic) sometimes, that's what we called it. But it was better than falling down, falling apart. That was over. We had done that already. This was now the 1940s and we three sisters were out. We had survived our own World War, like the one starting to rage in the whole world right now. We were here in New York City, and don't anyone forget that! But the boys, the three brothers we left behind in Catalina... Well, I'll tell you a little about the country they live in now.

In the time since my leaving Puerto Rey in 1939, President Galante was now not only a total dictator, but he had turned the country into a place we wouldn't recognize—militia was everywhere. Devotion had to be pledged to the President by every family—whatever that meant. Homes displayed his picture, next to God's. Businesses hung plaques that declared, "The Big G Governs Here." Citizens with political opinions were questioned at police precincts, so that ideas or talks *contra* (against) the President's decisions, could never be discussed in public. They called Galante the savior of our country. There was scandal talk too: that the President could take any woman he wanted, even if she belonged to one of his *politicos*. The worst thing was the talk about the young girls. A man sometimes was forced to pledge his loyalty by surrendering his tender daughter to *El Pulpo*, (The Octopus) as Galante was called.

I worried about the ugliness growing in my old home, but Rose was taking these worries to another level. In addition to the great hullabaloo of American activities Rose was involved in, her heart was deeply set inside her Puerto Rey. She had a group of Puerto Reyan friends in New York who I liked and respected very much. They visited our apartment on Sundays to drink coffee, smoke, and talk home politics. For hours they detailed the dangerous *precipicio* (precipice) that Puerto Rey was moving closer to. These friends were *simpáticos* but they scared me, because I had the feeling, they were not just talkers, but people who might want to do something. And Rose was one of them.

One night, straightening up after the Sunday company left, I found a box on the sofa with Rose's papers in it. There were newspapers on the coffee table too, mixed up with ashtrays full of cigarettes. I could always tell Rose's from the red lipstick on the ends. The newspapers were in Spanish and English, and a few in other languages. As far as I could tell, the circled articles were all about Puerto Reyan politics and especially about actions ordered by the government. Some were current, but several went back to the early 1930s.

I saw an article that described a labor strike settled by machine-gunning the gathered workers. Another paper told of a dissenting Puerto Reyan statesman who was eliminated by a grenade explosion. Several pieces described a ruthless genocide of African slave descendants living in Puerto Rey. Conducted on direct orders from the administration, the news stories said that hundreds were murdered by the military within a few days. I did remember hearing about some people who died during a farmers' rebellion—but not hundreds of people! I just couldn't believe this. I was still in Puerto Rey when this massacre supposedly happened.

My three brothers? This was the hell of a country we left them in? Thank goodness they managed to write letters to us. They were all living the lives of men now. Work, loves, marriage, adventures, misadventures, children, money, politics and the damn dictatorship filled their days. I came to realize that through and through, from the inside to the outside of our experiences, we sisters and brothers had always been the dictators' children—first *Papá's,* then Galante's.

Our Milo was living in a small country town of La Loma province, with his wife Fernanda and new babies that came almost every year. After four boys, Milo was still waiting for his little girls. I idolized my oldest brother as a child and did even now. Long ago, I used to make believe he was my father, instead of the General. Being 15 years older than me, seeing him like a young and gentle *Papá*, wasn't so hard to do. Milo looked just like our father: tall, thin, with extra-long arms and same color skin. But he was naturally kind. He was not a big talker, he was a deep knower, whether it was about his people or about important things in the world that he understood from reading law and history. The funny thing was that as much as Milo knew, he just put it away in his head and acted on the things his heart led him to do.

He called me *mi niña* (my girl) as a child and still addressed his letters that way to me. His messages were always like a father's: *"Acuerdate, mi niña, de lo que es lo más importante en la vida; el amor y la unidad de la familia. Cuando venga tu tiempo, elegir un hombre que sepa construir esto contigo. Nosotros crecimos bien alimentados, menos nuestros corazones."* (Remember, my girl, what is most important in life: the love and unity of family life. When your time comes, select a man who will know how to do this with you. We children grew up well-nourished, except for our hearts.)

But as much as Milo could be serious, he also filled his letters with funny stories about his everyday life—even the life he now lived under the dictatorship:

Our house, if you want to call it that, is like a long train that we keep on adding cars to, with more children. The only thing special about it is that it's off the town plaza. Right now, Big Galante, whose soul should be protected a thousand times by God, the angels, the saints, the ancestors and even the witch doctors and Babalu (just in case), is building a monument to himself with a fountain and bronze statue of his likeness in the plaza. I will not comment any further on this. However, I will tell you that my Fernanda has made herself a business by providing the construction workers with daily hot rolls in the mornings and cafecitos for their coffee break in the afternoons. May the great monuments to our Big Boy continue.

I want to also tell you that my schoolhouse, about which you know I am the teacher, principal, truant officer, and chief lice inspector, has recently received what I would call "advanced students." Galante's armed military men – I should say boys – occupy every town now, as part of the regular scenery. Two soldiers shyly came to the schoolhouse one afternoon and asked if I could show them how to read. Our ejército (army) receives thousands of poor, illiterate boys for whom military life is the only way upward in the Puerto Reyan world. And so, afraid to say no to any kind of government person, I agreed, and now spend lunch time teaching these muchachos (boys) their basics. I insist they leave their arms at the front door. The funny thing is, that naked of their rifles, they are as innocent looking as my own sons! Well mi niña, I must leave you now and say goodnight. It's late and I ring the school bell at eight a.m. Please receive the deepest love of your brother, Manuel Burgos Beltrán,—Milo

What we knew about our middle brother Dio was very little. It made me cry to think of his story—which I only understood in pieces. After about two years in the severe military academy *Papá* had sent Dio to for discipline, he escaped. He was 18 years old. For a long time, we had no idea where Dio was or how he lived. After he ran away, he would show up at the house about once a year, thin and sometimes dirty, asking for help. *Papá* refused to take him back. We children – by then, young adults – were so upset by our *Papá's* coldness.

Around the time Rose married Goya and Nina and I finished at the Teacher's College, Dio started to visit the house, looking a little better than usual. One evening, sitting with Papá on the front porch after having requested a real visit, Dio asked *Papá* for support. He had a good plan and a means of making a living this time. Somehow, he had learned how to tailor clothing very well. He asked *Papá* for 200 pesos to buy a portable Singer sewing machine, one he could take on the road to work in the small towns as a traveling tailor—a reasonable occupation at that time in our country. Our father, semi-happy with the idea, but afraid of the portable guitar and rum bottle Dio would *also* take on the road, finally gave him the money. For the last time in his life, Dio asked for his father's blessing.

"*¿Bendición, Papá?*" *Papá* made the sign of the cross on the boy's forehead and sent him on his way.

Our little brother managed to write us two letters after we moved to the United States. I guess he wrote these during times of being more stable—having a little money from his work and being with someone who gave him some sort of home or place. We were not sure if these were women or men. After the letters, though, I think times became very rough. I knew from the newspapers that Raúl Galante's government was especially cruel to men like Dio. I don't doubt the possibility that he may have spent time in jail. My brother, Dio is one of the tragedies of our family. He is one of our lost boys.

And then there was the last boy, Victor, the little prince as we used to call him. Rose and Nina didn't feel as angry as I did about our baby brother not growing up with us. We lost him as soon as he was born. The mistress ladies took him—yes, took him, and I'll never believe anything else. *Mamá* was dead, *Papá* was in hiding, and we were all in the boarding school. The ladies started minding the baby and never gave him back when we finally went home. Whoever heard of American teachers raising a Caribbean little boy, until he was a man? I will always be angry about that!

But I have to admit that I was very impressed by Victor when Nina and I went to say goodbye to him just before moving to New York. Victor, the man, was a very unique character—not like us, not funny like we were sometimes, just very serious. It was a seriousness inside

Victor that was not from being unhappy, but from the feeling that many things in our country and in the world, needed to be fixed. Like he had a responsibility for those things... I didn't understand this, it was something special in him. I think Victor's mothers, Miss Laura and Mrs. Wimble, managed to nurture our brother's soul so that he developed a passion for fighting cruelty against others. Along with his university diploma in accounting, our little brother was also completing training as a Methodist minister. Can you believe that? *Caramba*, shucks. I can't be critical of that. I hear that he preaches about human justice from the pulpit, in Spanish, as well as in perfect English without even the lick of an accent. Victor needs to watch what he says, though. President Galante's men, have been known to visit Sunday church services to assure that honor is paid to the Big G. Then, the most recent letter from our little prince carried a big surprise:

Dearest Sisters, I have met the young woman of my dreams. She is pure of heart and body, and faithful to the Christ who inspires all of our ways. Her name is Julia, and she will become my wife in four weeks. She is the one sent to be my life partner in preaching The Word in our country. We will be blessed with forming a large Christian family.
 I remain your faithful brother,
 Victor Burgos Beltrán

Although I thought my little brother sounded like a sixty-year-old holy man, I was excited for him. I thought it was a good sign that he wanted to make his own family after growing up away from his own. In his letter, Victor went on to say that he was working on fixing up a rented cottage that was not far from his mothers' school. This would be his first home as a family man with Julia.

Our hearts melted when we received any of our brothers' letters. We shared them, we devoured them, then read them all over again. On other days, though, I put my brothers away in a little closet of my mind (not quite into the deep ocean) because in 1940, Rose and I were flying, we were in love, and getting ready to take giant leaps into new lives.

Patti
20
American Bride
New York City, 1940

Rose and I were each getting married to our men. Our hearts were exploding. At least that's true for me. Rose was calmer in these months before her own marriage. We kidded her that she was, after all, a mature woman marrying for the second time. Had she grown out of the fantasy that after weddings, people lived happily ever after? I still believed that. So, I was ecstatic, and according to my girlfriends, looking prettier than they had ever seen me.

How there was the time to fall in love with Gabriel and spend hours with him talking about the lives we were going to have and the big family we were going to make, I don't know. I was working in our stores—two ladies' shops now; still studying English at night; and even taking classes for my U.S. citizenship test. I liked to think that I was on a great American carousel.

I probably knew Gabriel was going to be my husband from the first date we had. He came to pick me up at home as Rose had asked, meeting the sisters plus Rose's fiancé, Jorge, who was now part of the family. After toasting a small drink to new friendships, it was obvious Gabriel and Jorge were similar kinds of men: hard-working *caballeros* with easy smiles, who both idolized Mr. Heavyweight, Joe Louis. I watched Gabriel as he tried to show-off a little to my family without being too much. He was so proud about coming from Havana by himself and saving money by working almost every day of the week. In a few short months he would be co-owner of a luncheonette with his best friends and partners, Johnnie and his wife Angelita.

Gabriel obviously wanted to impress my family, but *ay*, enough already, I wanted to leave all of this conversation in our parlor and get on with the date. In America, didn't you have to go on a few of those before you got married? I was really, really surprising myself by being so definite about what I wanted. Me, Patti, with the fear of speaking my heart. Now I was *clara* (clear) about what I wanted. *Segura* (sure) about what was good for me. The more Gabriel opened himself to me, the surer I felt about who he was. On the intimate side, he never pushed me beyond a strong kiss, and I was grateful because I had no idea about what to do with either of our bodies. All I knew was that I wanted to be closer and closer to this man. Those *detalles* (details) I guess, would solve themselves in enough time. All my life I wanted a person who belonged to me, just to me.

After fourteen months of dating, we became engaged and our wedding was set. It was going to be a fancy party with a ceremony at Our Lady of Perpetual Help Church and a reception in the gala hall. Rose and Jorge were married six months earlier at New York's City Hall. Theirs was a tiny celebration at home with champagne and best friends. That Rose... she wanted to give me the big wedding, her little sister whom she understood had never had a mother to dress her for a party or tell her she was clever and lovely. Rose said, "Patti, *mi niña,* my girl with the sweet soul, I will make you a bride and give you a beautiful wedding because a mother does that."

And so, without asking me if I agreed with the plan – and I did – she became a tornado, making the entire bridal party's dresses in her shop. She said this task was the bridal order of her lifetime. We chose all of the fabrics together. There was the maid of honor's dress in slinky satin. That was Nina's, but she complained, "Jean Harlow is not my style, I can't wear that." There was the fluffy flower girl's dress, and the bridesmaids' dresses for my two best friends, Elizabeth and Fannie. They were crazy about their satin dresses. Finally, there was my dress.

"You know what looks good on me," I told Rose. So, she combined all the things I liked and that suited me. My dress was a dream. It was off-white satin, a little close to my body with a V neck and a real train. "Rosie, you really are my mother."

But inside of all the pre-celebrations, gifts and a bridal shower, something began to upset Nina. She was quiet a lot of the time, with a look that was either sad or mad. I really couldn't figure it out. Two short weeks before the wedding, I asked her to help me take some things over to my new apartment. Gabriel and I found a very cute one-bedroom place exactly one block from where we sisters were living. It was in a brownstone, as they called this kind of small apartment building, on the first floor, with windows facing the street. I always wanted a place with windows like that, where I could plant flowers and watch my neighbors go by. You entered right into the sunny living room. It had a little fireplace with green tiles around it. To the left was the kitchen with a brand-new gas stove. The bathroom with a bathtub inside was behind the kitchen. Right across the living room, separated by French paned double doors, was our bedroom. It was perfect!

So, on this day Nina walked over with me to my new place to help unpack new dishes and a toaster. Suddenly she started to cry, apologizing for not being happy enough for me.

"My problem," she said. "My problem is that we've never been away from each other. I've always felt like you were watching me, keeping me okay ever since we were little. What am I going to do now? You're the one who gets me to do things by laughing or something. Rose just gets impatient with me." Nina started to cry louder and shake all over.

Poor girl, what should I do? I just held her, and we sat on the sofa.

After a long time of crying, I got scared. Nina was saying things quietly to herself, not really talking to me. After about half an hour, I called Rose at the shop and asked her what to do.

"What is Nina saying to you now?"

"Rose, she keeps on repeating, with me sitting right there: 'I've lost Patti, I've lost Patti. You'll see, I've lost her.'"

Rose usually knew how to stop Nina's upsets, but instead she said, "Let's call Dr. Freudenberg, and I'll be right over."

Our family doctor was a small, round man with a thick German accent who made house calls until late at night. "I'll be there tonight," he said. "Put her to bed, keep her calm. One of you stay with her so she feels secure."

I knew what this was. I was secretly feeling it in these months of having Gabriel. I was Nina's chief defender, her interpreter. Now I was stretching my heart to love a man and make a new life with him. Did I have enough room inside me to love everything in my life? I couldn't take care of my little sister forever... What was wrong with her? Those feelings that she can't ever be separated from me... will that ever go away? Maybe it has something to do with the way we were separated from *Mamá* when we were tiny girls. Sometimes I think we're all children just making ourselves believe that we're grownups.

By the time Dr. Freudenberg arrived late that night, Nina was sound asleep with a hand curled around mine as I sat by the bed. Her lovely oval face and unblemished skin made her look like a girl. Over a Latin *cafecito*, which he never refused, the doctor answered questions Rose and I (and even *Papá*) had had for a very long time.

"What's wrong with her?"

"Your sister's mind works differently from ours," the doctor said. "On the one hand she has special intelligence: her unbelievable language talent, and that she can remember special details like the number of mosaic tiles in your lobby floor or the number of medical instruments in my office. I've talked to her over the time you've been my patients. She is a very, very interesting woman."

"But why is she so afraid?" asks Rose.

"*Ya, ya*, I'll get to that," he says with sad eyes. "But the other side of her is a child, a terrified child. Her ideas about frightening things could become very real to her someday. I know about what happened to you as children. It doesn't surprise me, Patti, that she's reacting to your moving away from her now."

"But Doctor, I love her, I'll see her every day if she wants me to."

"Nina will always be fragile," he says. "Maybe she'll need special care as the years go by. This is what is so." With this, the doctor finally said goodnight, leaving us to think about our sister's future and ours.

Learning about the deep things Nina felt turned my own head around. Why? Because it knocked me out of my silly young girl's idea that finding a man to love, and moving to the U.S., does not change everything in your world. According to the Doctor, I will always have a sister whom I love, who is not a regular person, and who might become even more confused and troubled in the future.

Rose and I did not speak after the doctor left. We hugged goodnight in our usual way, each deep in our own thoughts. We were exhausted. I realized that I was afraid now, for me *and* my Nina. How could I become a wife and make my own home when a sister of my heart would always need the attention of a child? As I walked into the bedroom that would soon be Gabriel's and mine, something inside me felt like thunder bolts in my head: they were words, screams, a strength of my own. "No. No. No. I'm not giving up my life. I'm not taking care of her. Did I say that? Did I really say that?" I love my sister. God, you know I love my sister. But she can't be my child. That's Rose's job!" And with that clear and hard declaration about our delicate Nina and our strong, golden Rose, our Rosina Dorada, I fell asleep.

The days went by, and my wedding day was almost here. I kept one eye on Rose's finishing my gown, and the other eye on Nina's mental state. She was the maid of honor so I tried to get together with her after work as often as I could to finish our planning. Using the excuses of needing to buy fancy hankies for the bridesmaids or more sweet almond candies for the wedding favors, we spent time shopping and going to dinner just like normal. I told Nina over, and over again – maybe too many times – how important a sister she was to me and that all the things we had suffered and enjoyed together would always bind our hearts, even though I would now be a married woman. Nina did become calmer, more her usual self. She even used her good fashion sense to suggest that a long strand of pearls would be perfect with the slinky, satin bridesmaid dresses. As for me, she lent me her new, double-strand pearl choker so that nothing would get in the way, she said, of showing off my beautiful dress.

My husband, my wedding, my family, and my Niagara Falls honeymoon were perfect. I was an American bride.

Patti
21
Patti and Gabriel
New York City, 1940–1947

Gabriel and I were a good couple. We had love and a lot of tenderness between us. Our little home was a shiny diamond that we polished and loved to decorate. Each of us worked hard, and now, after finishing payments for the diner in Jersey, we could really begin to save our money. We had great times with our friends and my family. Of course, there were problems, but the happy part was bigger – that's what was important.

"Let's put the new green chair by the window, so we can read there in the daylight," suggests Gabriel.

"Hmm, sure, but it needs something... like a nice table next to it where we can keep the newspaper and put an ashtray. Oh, and a cute vase for flowers."

"Okay, okay," moans Gabriel with a laugh. "*Querida*, darling, start getting ready. We're meeting Hilda and Bing at the Audubon at nine tonight."

"What? It's tomorrow, Saturday night."

"No baby, tonight is when the Chilean combo is playing for that *milonga*, the tango is going to be *fabuloso*.

I already shined my shoes. What are you wearing? Wear the sexy one with the slit in the back."

"Oh Gabriel, I haven't even done my hair." I ran into the bedroom and I'm ready in thirty minutes. I had a quick little thought, though, about how long it would take to get ready with a baby in the house, the baby we've been praying for for over five years. Oh well, I'm enjoying tonight. We're both going to be really *guapos* (good looking).

The Audubon Ballroom was on 168th Street and Broadway. We lived on 161st. This was a place for big events in upper Manhattan—concerts, political meetings, but most of, all dancing to big bands. It was a snowy night and, after dressing in all our finery, we had to put on sloppy galoshes over our precious dancing shoes—two clowns making faces in the long entry hall mirror. Gabriel and I were a funny pair. We were both kind of shy. I would say reserved. But put us together and we had the courage to do so many things and we could be pretty funny.

A cold Friday night in New York City is a serious thing, especially when you had to walk seven long city blocks in snow and wind blowing in from the Hudson. Imagine, I had on a lowcut cocktail dress under my coat— no sweater, of course. Even though I was wearing my new fur coat – Rose and I each bought one – I was freezing! By the time we got to the dance hall, we were a total mess. Gabriel's Rudolph Valentino hair was sticking up— naturally no hat, and my runny nose had wiped away all my red lipstick. We didn't care. This was the way we felt silly and happy. We saw Hilda and Bing right away checking in at the entrance. They looked worse than we did!

"Querida," Gabriel says. "You girls go fix yourselves up. Bing and I will check the coats and get us all a *palito,* a whiskey shot to warm up."

"Don't forget to settle down that hair," I tease Gabriel.

My friend Hilda was a beautiful woman with a child's round face that you wanted to squeeze every time you saw her. She was tender and kind, like the mother you would want to have. She and Bing were young marrieds like us who lived across the street—and our best friends. The great big difference was that they lived with Bing's mother without the privacy and fun of making a little home together. I knew this killed Hilda, but she was trying to hold on until they saved enough money to move out.

When Hilda and I got to the ladies' room, she said, "Patti, listen, I *gotta tell ya'*, I saw a specialist."

"What kind?"

"You know, the baby thing, someone who's an expert if you can't get pregnant."

"Really?" I say with big eyes.

"Yeah, yeah," says Hilda in her Brooklyn way. Hilda was born in Puerto Rico, but grew up in Flatbush—she *really* sounded American to me. "I'll tell *ya* all about it tomorrow. I'll come over for coffee in the afternoon. Oh, the band's starting up. Fix that lipstick and let's go."

Sliding on the big ballroom floor with Gabriel was always romantic for me. That night I danced without concentrating, just moving to the tango and making my leg kick through the slit in my skirt. Gabriel loved that, he thought it was really sexy. But my mind was actually a little upset—about what Hilda just told me. A specialist who could help her get pregnant? Gabriel and I had been trying for five long years, married already for almost six. We had seen doctors too, recommended by our Dr. Freudenberg, but nothing. In fact, we had just made a new plan to adopt a baby. This wasn't so hard to do if you're a loving couple, and we were; have a solid income, we had that; and knew people who could help you, we had that too. My family would be over the moon. But what was upsetting me was the news of Hilda's new doctor. Maybe there was one more chance for us to make a baby… But Gabriel was finished with that and the embarrassing examinations and pills. And actually, I'm ready for another plan too. Hilda's being so excited just made me jealous.

On our way home from the Audubon that night, the four of us walked down Broadway through tall mountains of snow. It wasn't that cold anymore, and the changing red and green traffic lights made the snow piles look like Christmas. We were happy and exhausted as we all hugged goodnight. Hilda and I both agreed to sleep in the next day and not meet for coffee till the following week. *Francamente* (frankly) I was relieved.

Oh, the weekends, we lived for them! And we didn't have a single one without doing something new. Together, we had double courage. Gabriel always slept late on

Saturdays, never working on the weekends. That was his deal with Johnnie. In exchange, he opened the diner every weekday morning. That meant taking the 4:03 train out of Penn Station to Perth Amboy, preparing the batters, baking the rolls and perking gallons of coffee for commuters going from Perth Amboy to Penn Station. He really worked hard—in fact, Gabriel was looking kind of tired lately. After running the diner for almost six years of our marriage, I heard him say for the first time that the schedule was feeling hard for him.

"What's going to happen when we have our baby? All those hours wasted on the train."

That conversation never progressed, but it made me think… Saturday mornings were also when we talked about our baby plans. We were waiting for our first interview with the Foundling Hospital after they approved our application to adopt an infant. We were so hopeful, and sure we could be good parents. "*Que sea lo que quiera Dios* (may it be what God wants), we would always say.

By noon on Saturdays, we were off to Rose, Jorge, and Nina's, for lunch and chatter about our week. Rose and Jorge always had news about their new ideas—we all had big dreams in those days. It was America, after all.

"Have you heard about what's going on in Miami? Most of it is swamp, but they're filling it up to make a great city. There are jobs, new houses. Maybe we could buy some land someday? And *compadres* (buddies), let's face it, the weather is *formidable*," said Jorge, blowing a kiss.

Rose's Jorge was a sweetheart. The best part was that he and Gabriel were such close friends. The "boys" dealing with the sisters!

Gabriel said, "We're staying right here. Once our baby comes, that little one will lead the way for our family of three. Who knows, they're building houses in New Jersey and Long Island like crazy – family houses with yards that could be perfect for us." I loved that my husband thought this way.

PART III
Maritza

Maritza
22
Family of Two
New York City, 1947–1948

Like the sparkling miracle that it was, Patti and Gabriel gave birth to their own healthy baby girl the following year. Like the pit of darkness the world became, Gabriel died suddenly of a fatal heart attack, sixteen weeks after their child was born. Patti turned to stone, plummeting deep into her ocean. Death annihilates those it leaves behind. The American bride in the American dream was gone in a heartbeat.

    I am Patti and Gabriel's child. They named me Maria Stelladora, the namesake of my aunts, Rosina Dorada (Rose) and Nina Maria (Nina), and my grandmother, Estrella. But Gabriel nicknamed me Maritza in the weeks he lived as my father. It's a lighthearted name, happy and playful, like a song. Maybe Gabriel wanted to leave me with a melody before he died. I don't know. It's just what I have of him.

Gabriel and Maritza at 4 months

Gabriel and Maritza

We are both dressed in our Sunday best
You in your dark suit and linen shirt
Me in my brimmed bonnet and sweater
Knitted by the Little Sisters of the Sacred Heart.

You've just stuffed your white hankie into your suit pocket
After wiping some dribble from my chin.
I wear the clothes of a cherished child,
You wear the polished shoes of a *caballero*.

We are a family of three, out on a Sunday walk.
We love who we are.
We stop for a photo before strolling to Riverside Park.
Mommy takes the picture of her two jewels.

Fifty hours later, on Tuesday evening,
We become a family of two.
Your heart stops as you bend over my crib.
Hold my glasses, Patti, you say.
I'm falling.
And you did.
And you died.

What I want to know is

What happened between us from Sunday afternoon to Tuesday evening?
Did we talk?
Did you rock me to sleep?
Did you tell me about your day at the diner?
In those fifty hours
Were you able to fit in the love that would have to last me for a lifetime?

The biggest question I've had all my life is how my father would have loved me if he'd lived. I'll never know but for the fantasies of a child, or those of an adult woman trying to conjure the image of someone who never existed for her. Yes, there were those first sixteen weeks. But that has never been enough to go on. So, Gabriel remains a figment to me, a story of a kind, a handsome and lovely man who adored his wife, loved Latin ballroom dancing, dressed elegantly, owned a diner, and smoked Lucky Strikes. He combed his black hair slicked back in the style of the day. He has floated through my dreams all my life, an ephemera, an illusion, a not-flesh father, my mother's ghost-husband. As an adult, I have sometimes dabbled in the whispers of the afterworld, trying to convince myself that Gabriel moves around my life.

Smoke

I love being alone in my house.
It's a dreamy place that sits in the middle of a pasture.
Some days I study the paintings on my walls.
Every line, every hue, every stroke of sorrow and mirth drawn by the artist.
On the far wall is the portrait of a gypsy boy playing a guitar.
He loves the shock of black hair that covers his left eye.
By the window hangs the Russian bride.
She is bejeweled and flashes hazel eyes as she awaits her beloved.

Then, in the midst of this, I smell it.
Cigarette smoke.
It moves like a ribbon in the air.
It's above me, slipping down toward my shoulder.
It's behind me now, moving round to touch my face.
A millisecond makes it disappear
Smooth as satin,
Moving by its own heartbeat
My father is here.

I have a lot to tell. It's hard—thus the poems to share my deepest places. I feel tired even before I begin. I've always lived with a cacophony of voices inside me. They are dreams about what would have been if Gabriel had not left me so early; they are whispers about the lives of my Caribbean kin. They shape the way I experience the world.

When Gabriel died, Patti fell into her ocean. She drowned—almost. She became the smallest, quietest version of young Petra, the child, who had ever existed. Her love, her reason for being, her Gabriel, was gone. But there was the baby.

I don't know when it happened; it was probably early. It could have been in the cradle, or on our walks, or when she told me stories: I came to know my mother's inner mind very well. What a keen student I was! I had to be. What I mean is, I learned to swim in her underwater, her murky ocean of silent, swimming ghosts. I learned how her ghosts had loved her, abandoned her, and haunted her. No words, I just knew. I knew by the way she took care of me: her thousand kisses, her long goodnights, her cooing rhymes, her blank stares, her making my clothes, her pushing food, her paranoid sightings, her demands I smile. And there was her fear of fire, her death by silence, her terror of the ocean, her dainty dressing, her fear of men, her abhorrence of violence. She never left me alone except for much later when, from nine to three in the afternoon, I was under the protection of the school nuns. From my mother's caring hands flowed the tender, tragic stories of her own life.

Patti loved me deeply and desperately. I understood why. She didn't want to lose her only good thing. For Patti, her child meant love and that was a reason for her life.

What do you expect from a person who lost their own mother at the age of three; normal love? But I believe it was my father Gabriel's sudden death that finally put my mother into a strange, altered state of being. By the time Galante murdered her brother and cousins later in the 1950s, she was already gone. The young woman who was the perky immigrant newcomer and American bride, disappeared. That makes me so sad. How many loves can leave you before you change who you are? After mourning scars heal, what is left is a self that is remade. I have always understood that about her.

So, Patti created her new *razon para vivir* (reason for living): to be the axis around which I, her child, pivoted, spun, and developed. That axis was fixed in stone. Unmovable. Nothing else really mattered to her. For me the upside of this arrangement was that being the apple of someone's eye, and that of the family's as well, meant I had it good from the very beginning of life: loads of love, great toys, good schools, bags of Bazooka, pretty clothes, tickets to the Howdy Doody show. The downside was – let's face it – who's ever going to adore you that way again? And besides, there's the thorny problem of that axis arrangement – I could only spin around so far. That radius became excruciatingly short, once I started to leap and spin and grow. When I became twelve, all hell broke loose. I found a way to disassemble the axis arrangement – not out of cruelty, I don't think, or bad intention, but with the simple desire to stretch as far as I could possibly grow. I needed to renegotiate that arrangement fast, so I could grow farther and taller and more intricate than Mom ever imagined. I had to step beyond the fatherless baby, beyond the care of the widowed bride. I had to eventually go my way.

Maritza
23
Patti and Maritza
New York City, 1948–1952

In my life with Mom, I was a deeply thinking and feeling child from very early on. The family story goes that just after my father died, my mother lost her marbles, dropped her basket, as they used to say in the early parlance of misunderstood grief. On the morning after my father's funeral, she disappeared with me, leaving a note for her sisters. "I have to be alone with my baby. I need to figure out what to do. I can't think with all of you around me. Don't look for me. I'll be okay. Love, Patti."

After a few days of frantic searching, a call came for Rose from cousin Zoraya, telling her that Mom and I were staying with her and safe. She said we slept together most of the day except when we were both howling. Patti only came out of our room to warm a bottle.

During these long, dark days I, a baby, began to actually think and speak—all in my mind, of course. I thought: "Staying in this room isn't really good for us, we've got to get out, have some fresh air." So, I started turning my head toward the baby buggy parked by the closet in our room. Patti finally said, "Let's go for a walk, baby, it's stuffy in here." For the first time since the day of the funeral, Mom got dressed. She put on a pretty Sunday outfit and decorated me in one of my mohair sweaters and brimmed hats. And so, after days in our cocoon, Mom and I stepped out.

The fresh air felt great. It was strange outdoors. I was on my back in the carriage, tucked in tightly with a blanket. The little bumps of the carriage wheels on the pavement and curbs tickled my stomach. I didn't move, but stared upward with giant eyes, at the sky, the light, the tall apartment buildings whizzing past my view. So, this was the outside world without Gabriel? So far, it looked the same to me. I was okay and comfortable. Mom? Well, all I knew was that my carriage trembled when she stood at street corners to wait for the green light.

Mom began to take a stroll with me every day. We mostly walked along Broadway, sometimes Audubon Avenue, from around 154th Street where Our Lady of Perpetual Help Church was, to 181st Street where there were great shoe shops and Wertheimer's Department Store. We passed by a lot of places familiar to Mom. She called them out as we went by, "This is our Rose's Dress Shop, the Columbia Presbyterian Hospital where you were born, the RKO Theater with Saturday double features, and the Bickford Cafeteria—where we had lunch before the movies." At some point, Mom added Rose, Jorge and Nina's apartment building to the route. We never walked past our own apartment which was only one block away. Mom said: "Maritza, should we move in with our family so we won't be alone?" I didn't know how to say "yes" yet.

All I knew was that returning to our room at Zoraya's place sucked us back into the place where there was no beginning or end, no day or night. I thought, "What if my mother keeps me here forever and I never get out to become the person I need to be?" It was a place called sadness. We screamed together, ate together, slept together. After weeks of this, I started to go out of my mind! Get me out of here!

Suddenly one day, Mom stopped crying. This was my chance. I continued to cry and cry and cry, over many nights. Mom had no choice but to desperately unplug herself from me. At 2:32 in the morning, exactly forty days after my father's death, my mother called Rose and blurted out, "Can baby Maritza and I live with you?"

Rose said, "We'll pick you up right now."

And so began my life as the luckiest baby in northern Manhattan. My family was an unusual crew of five adults. I had a dead father and four parents: a mother who over adored me, two doting aunts and an uncle – Rose's husband Jorge – who was my daddy's best friend. What else could a baby want? You can't have everything… And my mother's clinging to me—let's just say the family helped me get some air sometimes.

Mom began to change as soon as we settled into our family's apartment. I was so relieved. She was almost back to her old self from when my dad was around. How long is mourning supposed to last? I saw her trying to be as normal as possible, like a person who didn't just have her husband disappear. Mom put her biggest effort into taking care of me. She was actually cheerful, hummed and played and sang to me, loving to dress me in pretty clothes. She chatted with me about everything—except my father. A strange thing, right? In our room, I heard her cry at night, so I knew she missed him. But she never told me about that. I got the message we were now supposed to make believe he never existed. Life was going to be our lives right now, what Mom created for us. I think our past with my dad Gabriel is gone.

Mom created a very special normal for us. There were daily walks to Riverside and Pigeon Park, and playgroups during the winter. My mother had lots of good friends with kids and dads, as if to show me what a regular family was supposed to be like. She helped friends in a pinch so kids were around for me to play with—as if she wanted to show me what siblings were supposed to be like. Within these silent lessons, she never mentioned my father.

And then there was my Uncle Jorge. I learned to walk early so I could follow him around the house, giggling and happy. Mom set up the time after dinner for he and I to have a *conversation*—as if to show me what a father at home is supposed to be like. Mom tried to fill the holes in my life. My father Gabriel had no part in this project except as the ghost she wanted me to forget.

Outside of Mom and me, the world of family activity buzzed. Rose had different kinds of businesses now. She wasn't in the tailoring business anymore. "An immigrant's job," she said. She now had a stylish ladies' shop, as well as a children's clothing store. Mom returned to work when she didn't feel so sad anymore and managed Rose's children's shop. Jorge graduated from dental technical school and was opening a business that made false teeth. Rose and Jorge were the new all-American couple who loved talking about this land of opportunity. They had big dreams. "Si Señor, yes sir, Florida is the place to be. We're going as soon as we save enough to buy some land," said Jorge in his big Spanish accent.

By the time I was two, I started to understand that my family spoke two different languages, and that there were rules about when to speak each of them. In the outside world they spoke English, just like everyone else in our neighborhood, in the stores, on the bus. The sisters all spoke pretty well because when they were girls, they went to an American school, where the mistresses taught them. Spanish was not allowed outside the house because everyone was trying to behave like a regular American— and this also meant being on very good and polite behavior when you were in public. They told me to behave and never whine outdoors. But inside the house, our family spoke Spanish. Spanish was the best talk because everyone laughed and was funny and even yelled at each other that way. I learned how to speak Spanish very fast because they loved that, so I went around saying, *"te quiero, Tío, te quiero, Mami"* (I love you, uncle, I love you, Mommy). They hugged and kissed me when I did that. The best one was "*Bambi, venga!*" Bambi was my dog, a beagle, and when I said that, he was ready to play. But when we took him out for a walk I said, "*Bambi, come.*" It was the only thing I knew how to say in English for a very long time.

I was five when I started kindergarten at the local Catholic School of the Holy Family. From the first day I didn't like the scratchy uniform jumper and white blouse. But my schoolbag was great: navy blue with brown leather trim, and Snow White with the dwarves painted on the front. Being with other children was okay for me, from all the play activities my mother took me to, but nothing prepared me for the hundreds of noisy children lined up in the schoolyard. And there were these people – birds – no robots – no, ladies, dressed in black and white veils. What were they?

All of a sudden, I was climbing up some stairs with other children. One of the big lady birds was in front of us and when I turned to look and look, my mother was not behind me. A feeling started from deep inside my stomach to the top of my head. I was going to explode. But I remembered my mother saying to me firmly, "Only speak English in school." But how do you say in English: "*Ayyyyyy. Que pasa aquí? Donde está mi Mami*?" (What's happening here? Where is my Mommy?) I settled for freezing on the stairs and screaming. Children were telling me to move. The big lady bird – they called her a nun – came down and lifted me, so my cheek rubbed against her black veil. I liked the way she smelled. She was kind and whispered, "I'm Sister Mary Lawrence." When we got to the classroom, she seated me at the table right next to her desk. There were three other children at this table. I liked the little chairs. But I was still crying and everyone was speaking crazy English. I understood them. But I had none of my own English words for them.

I was silent and stared at others with nothing to say. I was alone. As months went by in this big sunny classroom with giant windows, I learned colors and numbers and how to line up for the bathroom just like everyone else. I understood the rule that writing on a page goes from the left side to the right side of the notebook. I understood that you didn't turn around during morning prayers. But I still had no words. Sometimes when I was tired, I thought of my mother's face. How do you say, "I want to go home now?"

One day when the snow was falling outside of our big windows, Sister Lawrence asked, "Children, what do you call the time when it snows and it's cold outside?"

I raised my hand and said, "Winter."

Maritza, age 5, School of the Holy Family

Maritza
24
My New World
Miami, Florida, 1952–1954

There was trouble in the house with my Aunt Nina. She was one of my favorite people in the world. But the rest of the family was always mad at her for... something. Maybe it was that she kept her room piled high with boxes filled with her things; or that she wouldn't let anyone come in to clean. She taught me big words in English, and because of her, I was the best speller and reader in the School of the Holy Family's first grade. *Disheveled,* she taught me. "That just means sloppy, what your mother calls my room." *Frustrated,* she called herself. "That means you want to give somebody a punch in the nose."

I laughed and laughed when she said this because Nina, who was a tall, elegant, very quiet lady, made a fist and punched the air with a funny face. We also had little secrets. Like letting me try on her jewelry or filling up one of her boxes with my dolls. But even though I loved and got along with Nina, in my child's mind, I knew there was something different about her, different from the rest of the family. I heard her having conversations in her room when she was alone.

Something bad happened at Nina's job and so, she wasn't going to work anymore. At night when I was trying to fall asleep in my room, I heard the grownups talk in the kitchen. That's how I found out about everything. I heard words about Nina like "too much stress" (*nerviosa)* and "not a normal person." I hated my family for saying things about Nina. I loved her.

Another thing I heard from the night kitchen was even more important: Rose and Jorge were moving to Florida—wherever that was. And they wanted Mom and me to move with them. My mother sounded strange when she talked to them about it, like she was either going to yell at them or start crying.

"Florida?" she whined. "It's, it's like the country there! Palm trees, sloppy people, and dark at night with no streetlights. Our family belongs together and in the city!"

"Honey," says Rose, "Our family does belong all together. You'll see, you'll like it for Maritza and you. You'll have a car. You can study and work at whatever you want. You'll have financial security. We bought two houses right next to each other. Perfect. Your house is an adorable cottage, blue with white trim, and it's right across the street from the grammar school. Jorge and I have great chances for buying more property there. And think of our Nina. Let's face it. We know she's not well. Maybe the weather will help her."

"But, but," babbled Mom.

My mother, Patti, sounded just like me, a little girl whose family was forcing her to do something. Rose was the bossy mother. And Patti was mixed up between Rose's great ideas and feeling mad at being told what to do. I had figured this out about my mother and Rose's relationship.

One year later after finishing first grade, Mom and I did move to Florida to be with our family. Behind her smiles and positive talk about our move, Mom was scared. As for me, I thought anything with an airplane ride had to be super and terrific. And besides, to be with Rose, Jorge and Nina again meant that my cocoon with Mom might not hold me in so much.

I noticed the change as soon as we walked out of the Miami Airport. A whoosh of air that was damp and full of the sun, hit me in the face. I never smelled anything so delicious in my life. I wanted to take a bath in it. I yanked off my silly straw hat and sweater and said, "Mom, take my purse too. It's hot, my face is wet, I want to put on shorts."

Rose and Jorge finally found us. Uncle ran up and swung me, laughing, into the air like he always used to. Mom and *Tía* hugged and kissed and cried all the way home. Home was now Aunt Rose's ocean-blue house with white doors and windows. There were big red rose bushes in the front yard that Uncle had planted especially for her. And the very front of the house had tall palm trees with big, round, smooth trunks that stood like soldiers guarding the front porch. The house for Mom and me was right next door, blue and white too, just smaller. The men were working on it inside and outside so we couldn't go in yet, but it was going to belong to us.

The inside of Rose and Jorge's house was cool and quiet and smelled like Aunt Rose's cooking.

"Where's Aunt Nina?" I said it loud so she could hear me.

"Shh, shh," Rose and Jorge say at the same time. "She's resting. She had a headache today."

I didn't like that answer. I really wanted to see her, so I laid on my stomach in the hall right up against her bedroom door and whispered, "Nina, Nina, it's me, Maritza. I'm here now, I'm here."

No answer.

You'll see her at dinner," says Aunt Rose, "Come, I have a surprise for you."

Standing in the middle of the living room was a blond, round, curly-haired little girl who looked about my age. "This is Pam, Maritza, she lives right next door. She wants to play with you."

"Let's go," Pam says. "I'll show you my back yard. Call me Pammy, it's prettier. I have two big brothers who never play with me. I play the accordion. I practice every day. That's why I have a round belly, so I can rest it there."

"Really?" I say.

Pammy's backyard was right next to Aunt Rose's. Big mango trees were everywhere, making the yards shady and cool. And on the ground were around a thousand yellow mangoes. We got a big tin from Pammy's house and collected loads of them.

"Here's how you eat a mango—you pound it and squish it, then bite a hole at the top so you can suck the sweet insides out."

We sat on my new friend's kitchen step and ate a hundred mangoes.

"Boy, are we a mess—there's yellow mango juice all over us!" Then Pammy said, "Let's go, Maritza. Just lick your fingers and wipe them on your dress, I want to show you something."

So, I followed my new friend and we ran down the block and across the road where there was a place that looked like a jungle. There were coconut trees with vines winding all around them, and giant purple flowers with yellow brushy things popping out. But behind the jungle, it was different. There were rows and rows of big red strawberries. I had never seen strawberries growing in the ground before. We picked and ate berries and they were warm. "From the sun," Pammy said.

All of a sudden, a man's grumpy voice yelled, "Hey you kids!"

Pam said, "Run," so we ran across backyards, over a concrete wall, and landed in someone's patio. Pammy said, "Oh, this is Loreen's house." So, she knocked at the side door and a very old grandma answered, saying Loreen went clothes shopping with her mother. When the grandma closed the door, Pammy whispered, "Loreen is spoiled: she gets everything she wants."

When we turned to leave, I noticed that we'd been out for a long time. The day was changing, and the sky was blue and orange now. I didn't know where I was. I felt like I'd been out on a long trip with this funny Pammy girl who didn't stop talking or going wherever she wanted to go.

As we got close to our street, I heard people in my family calling me. "Mariiitza, Maria Stelladooora." When my mother saw me, she came running. She was crying and really mad. She grabbed my arm and gave me a swat on the behind. "Don't you ever, ever go anywhere without telling me. And in a city, we don't even know yet! *Caramba* (Darn it), we just got here an hour ago!"

"But Aunt Rose told me to play with P…"

"I'm the boss of you. You hear me? No one gives you permission to do anything except me!"

I was in big trouble. I came to dinner after getting cleaned up and stayed quiet. I kept my eyes down because that's what you did in *respeto* (respect) with your family when you were punished. But I wasn't sad, because I did something for the very first time alone, without my mother, just with myself. I loved it here! Miami was going to be good! My Nina was at the table. She gave me a little wink.

As time went on, so many more things were good. I had such a long list. I wore sandals or went barefoot. Mom hated that. I ran between our houses and yards all day long. I met two cute sisters, Linda and Ellen, who lived around the corner. After begging Mom for weeks, she let me take lessons at the same tapdancing studio the sisters went to. And soon, we little girls put on funny shows for our families in the backyard. Pammy, of course, had to be the opening star on her accordion.

I loved my family. Sometimes Aunt Rose took me to her real estate office. Her new job was called a real estate agent—and she let me be a secretary. And Nina, who mostly sat alone in her room, saved her conversation for me. But the best thing was, I was my Uncle Jorge's pal. He said, "C'mon kid," and we were on our way in the car to get gas, or buy a big kingfish at the Miami pier for company. Uncle Jorge was a carpenter for big store windows. He could make anything, even pretty furniture and decorations for Rose. When we were out driving and saw some important junk left on a street corner, we snuck up and put it in the car trunk really quick so no one saw us. Rose yelled at *Tío* when he brought this stuff home.

"Que verguenza. ¿Y si alguien que conosemos los ve? (How embarrassing. What if someone we know sees you two?) We're property owners now!" She was only make-believe mad. I could tell, because she would tell the story about what we did, laughing to my mother. Oh, and another thing about Uncle Jorge was that he had a "making false teeth business" too in a tiny room off the kitchen. I thought it was a little disgusting when his customers came over and had their new teeth put in at the dining room table with the lace tablecloth. Yuk, didn't *Tío* know about their saliva?

Three blocks from our houses was the Miami Bay. Aunt Rose taught me the streets in case I ever got lost. To go there, you crossed South Miami Avenue, then Brickell

Avenue, then the Bay. It was beautiful and cool at night. Sometimes we took a walk there after dinner. Everyone came, even Nina, who walked Dickie, the family sausage, I mean dachshund. He was taffy brown and barked as soon as he smelled the fishy smell by the Bay. My mother and aunts always looked so pretty on these walks, wearing their flowery cotton dresses—clothes that ladies of their country, Puerto Rey, changed into after cooking and before dinner, so they were fresh for the evening. Uncle Jorge had his own little habit in the evening, too. After kissing all the ladies when he came home from work, he went to the pantry and poured one *palito* (shot) from whatever liquor was there. Then he went inside for a hot shower and a clean shirt. "I'm a new man," he yelled when he came out. Then he went into the kitchen to peek at what was cooking.

But the best nights, even better than the Bay, were driving to the beach after dinner. No one was there except for us, and the sand and the ocean. Mom and Nina usually didn't come to the night-beach with us. These times I made believe Jorge was my father and Rose was my mother, and we were our own little family. Was that bad? We always joked that the ocean was as warm as being in a bathtub, so when I went home, I told Mom I wouldn't need a bath before bed. On these nights I slept for a long time with very sweet dreams.

After some months in Miami, I began to see that my mother was not happy. She told me I was becoming wild, and that I paid more attention to Aunt Rose than to her.

"Oh Mami, why do I see you be sad when I'm so happy? I'm still loving you, but it's just that I'm busy now. There are lots of things to do, so many other people to love."

Mom took good care of us. She fixed up our house, helped me with school projects. We took the bus together when just the two of us went out to investigate Miami. On Sundays, she and I walked around the downtown and had lunch in restaurants with tables outside that had pretty umbrellas. I loved to eat there. We discovered a Chinese store where *Mami* bought me something every time we went—colored fans or a little paint set with brushes. She seemed happier on Sundays. Sometimes we had dinner at a restaurant, where I think the waiter liked her. One time he gave her a flower, and he treated us a little special. I noticed that she behaved a little differently when we went there. She always looked nice and smoked a Kool cigarette with her coffee. The waiter would light it for her.

When we got home, I begged to run over and tell the rest of the family what we did on our exploration. She usually told me it was late, not to go, and I saw something happen on Mami's face—like her smile from the day went away. It's the same way she looked when she told Aunt Rose, that Miami was a lonely place for her, and that it was hard to make friends. Rose told Mom that she has to *seguir paralante* (move forward with herself) and not act like *la pobre viuda*. I asked Nina what this meant, and she said my mom acted like "the poor, lonely widow."

I still didn't get it. All I knew for sure was that the more I did with Rose and Jorge and Nina and my new friends, the more unhappy Mami seemed to get. There was something else too. It was Nina. I know I'm just a kid, but I felt that Mom was a little afraid of her now. She didn't visit Nina's room much, and she wasn't sweet with her anymore. How could my mother be afraid of her own sister? Aunt Rose wasn't.

Still, I knew that Aunt Nina was really different now. She talked a lot more to herself, yelled a little bit too, like she was arguing with somebody. I missed her coming to dinner, so we brought her a tray. I couldn't explain it, but even though she did strange things, she was still my Nina. Mom seemed to move further and further away from her. Nina showed me where she hid her little diamond earrings and her mother Estrella's ruby ring. I knew where she kept her secret sealed envelopes.

"Don't tell anyone," she whispered. "This is just in case something happens to me."

"Okay, Nina, okay, Nina. I know, now tell me one of your ideas, tell me something you know about."

You see, Aunt Nina knew special things about the world because she was very smart and maybe had a little magic too. I believed everything she said. I think. Something about her face and the way she walked made me think of her as a brilliant Duchess.

The best thing about Nina, though, was how much she loved me. She told me that I was the most beautiful thing in her world. On one hot night, we were sitting in the front yard under the palm trees after walking Dickie. Nina said it was the perfect time to show me the night stars that would tell my future. I didn't really understand this, except that it had something to do with me as a grownup, and I really wanted to know about that. But our special time together was broken all of a sudden, because my mother rushed out and ordered us inside. I had to go right to bed. Did my mother think that too much time alone with Nina was not a good thing?

I stopped believing in the magic of my Duchess, when she disappeared from home a few weeks later. Nina, who almost never left her room, was gone, gone for three long days. Our family finally found her walking far from home, in the Miami heat, wearing her fur coat, and carrying a kitchen knife in her purse. I watched from our car as Uncle Jorge and two policemen gently placed Nina inside an ambulance. Aunt Rose explained to me that there was something sick inside Nina's mind and that she was going to a hospital that would make her better. My mother especially did not want to hear any talk from me about my Nina's mind being perfectly fine. Mom became even sadder if I talked about Nina, kind of like when I asked her anything about my father.

I had a lot of questions about all this. Could you be sick in your mind and still be smart? Could you be sick in your mind and still love people? I didn't know yet.

Maritza
25
The Puerto Reyans
Miami, Florida; Catalina, Puerto Rey, 1950s

There were some secrets happening in Aunt Rose's house, that were scary. *Mami* didn't even want to know, and when certain people came to visit, she made sure we weren't around—like on Sundays when we went out for the day. But sometimes I was sitting in the kitchen doing my homework or running by the porch where the visitors sat, so I heard things. They talked, talked, talked about *política* (politics) and Puerto Rey and sometimes they cried, "*Horror, horror.*" I heard: "*No podemos seguir asi.* (We can't go on like this)." And I've heard the name Raúl Galante many times. I asked *Mami* who this was, and she told me never to mention that name—it was a dangerous person. In general, Mom always kept me away from hearing about or seeing anything rough or nasty. She wouldn't even let me stay in the living room if there was boxing on television.

I had cousins in the Puerto Rey, who I had never met. They belonged to Uncle Milo, the sisters' oldest brother, and Uncle Victor, the youngest brother who was raised by the American ladies. Milo had ten children; can you imagine? And only two of them were little girls. I wished I could know them. I wished they were my sisters. We could live together here in Miami and go to school, and then play by the fruit trees afterward. Mom told me Uncle Milo's family lived deep in the country, and he was the only teacher of the only school in their town. And Uncle Victor—isn't it funny they used to call him baby Victor? He lived in the capital city of Catalina, and had four children. My favorite was Anita because she was a girl and my age. I talked to her on the telephone once. She said hi to me in English. I loved her. I wanted her to be with me. Maybe someday we'll be together, and I could teach her how to tap dance. I'm the only kid in my little family. Sometimes it's not fun.

Today we got a letter from Uncle Victor in Puerto Rey. Mom read it out loud to everyone after dinner. I didn't really understand all of it.

Mis queridas hermanas (my dear sisters):

It gives me both joy and sorrow to write, as I yearn to see your beautiful faces and feel the warmth of your hearts. We are as well as we can be in a country that is training us to be exemplary citizens. Now we are totally entwined with the motherland – "nuestra patria." We are told that all our labor, the raising of our families, the commitments to our government, are ordained by God. And the symbol of the Almighty in Puerto Rey is our leader, Raul Galante, to whom we must pay homage and obedience every day of our lives. As a Minister, I have orders to preach this message every Sunday in my church. Our family is trying its very best to be good citizens. Given that we now live in the capital city on a block where some military officers also live, we make sure to keep our yards in perfect order. We have placed, as now is the custom, a large portrait of our leader above our entry door. And we are teaching the children to say, "Que viva Galante," (Long live Galante) whenever they greet an adult.

I am trying to be correct. Our beliefs in this regime must be beyond scrutiny. We are instructed to examine our consciences for any signs of negative feelings against the "Great Leader" and his policies. Sometimes we are called into administration offices and offered assistance with our examinations, for a few hours—or a few days. "Dios gracias" (thank God) I feel myself a fortunate man to be working directly for the government in my weekday position at the International Trade Division. This way, I serve my country in its forward progress, as well as our Presidente, in his burning desire for the growth of our Puerto Reyans...

Un fuerte abrazo para Jorge. Están todos en mi corazón. Su hermano, Victor Burgos Beltrán

A strong embrace for Jorge. You are all in my heart.
Your brother, Victor Burgos Beltrán

There was total silence in the room when *Mami* finished reading the letter. My Uncle Jorge was the first to speak, stretching out his arms and shaking them like he did whenever he got upset. He started quietly, then began to raise his voice, "What, what? You know what he's saying? That the country is a military state. He has to preach government propaganda every Sunday! People are brought into precincts for questioning if they're suspected of not being with the regime. Questioning? Ridiculous! Rose, Rose, he means beating! What he didn't say is that those who are kept for days may never come back—you hear me? *Se desaparecen, mi amor...* (Gone, they disappear, darling)! Oh my God, Rose. We've got to do something. Get them out of there. Preach Galante propaganda in church? Did you hear that?"

"Jorge, calm down," says Rose. "There are people working on this. You know that."

"Quiet! Quiet! Close the door," says Jorge. "Are you out of your mind mentioning that in the open, woman?"

My mother was really nervous with the conversation now and said firmly, "It's bedtime, Maritza. Let's let the grownups talk. *Buenas noches* everybody. Say goodnight."

I was scared, walking over to our little house, but I didn't know why. I was confused about what the grownups were talking about tonight. I finally got to sleep after *Mami* gave me a warm glass of milk. And then I had this dream:

I'm on a long ladder that goes down, down into a stinky cellar where there is something hidden. There isn't much light, and I'm scared of the spiders. When I get to the end, there's a hole in the ground with another ladder going down. How far, how far, I cry? I scream in my sleep, and then my mother wakes me and says, "Shh, you're okay, you're home, *mi niña*. It's the middle of the night here in Miami, 3.24 a.m. Go back to sleep now."

At the very same time of 3:24 am in Catalina, Puerto Rey, Victor Burgos Beltrán (Maritza's uncle and Rose, Patti and Nina's youngest brother) is awake in his home and climbing down the wooden stairs that lead to his sub, sub cellar. It is the place where he has a small, secret printing shop, known to no one but his sixteen-year-old son, Victor Jr. and the four other men in los Águilas, (the Eagles), his clandestine cell. They are a tiny part of a large network trying to overthrow Dictator Galante's regime. Victor's job is to prepare a new front page for the next day's newspaper. It will have new headlines and photos displaying the most recent state-sanctioned violence: "Twenty-three University Students Detained and Disappeared" "Military Sets Fire to Shantytown as Two Hundred Left Homeless." As many newspapers as possible will be replaced with the new front cover. In the morning, men from the cell carry these "new" newspapers into town, casually leaving them on a bus or park bench—sometimes even at the entrance of a government building.

The purpose of Victor's secret cell is simple: Puerto Reyans need to know that their government is a terrorist state. In the 1950s, the tyranny of the Galante dictatorship turned ordinary men and women into underground operatives. Hundreds of secret cells like Victor's disseminated forbidden information and strategized toward a final end. Cells consisted of only a handful of people. A participant knew the person who gave him a direct order, and the person she/he subsequently gave an order to. This was a safeguard in case of capture.

I was still very sleepy when I got up in the morning after my scary dream. Even though *Mami* tried to calm me down, I didn't sleep because I kept on thinking of someone hurting me in a dark place. *Mami* asked me to tell her the dream at breakfast. I told her. She said, "It's just a bad nightmare, darling. Try not to think about it. If it comes into your mind, remember that your Father God is walking right alongside you."

Maritza
26
Just Like Topsy
Miami, Florida, 1950s

Our homes in Miami were in a really pretty part of the city, surrounded by big shady trees and beautiful flowers. Our family made lots of friends with our neighbors, but most of them didn't speak Spanish like we did. I'm going to tell you some things that happened to me and *Mami* in Miami. Everything that happened added up to my mother having an explosion that changed my whole life.

One day Uncle Jorge came home a little later than usual, looking upset and kind of messy. He told us some men beat him and threw him off the bus because he gave his seat in the white people's section to a black woman holding a baby. In Florida, the buses were strange. White, light-skinned people sat in the front, and dark-skinned, colored people sat in the back. Uncle Jorge said that it was *un crimen* (a crime) to make a tired woman stand because there were no seats left in the colored section. Uncle said somebody had to do the right thing, get up, and give her a seat. When he did, some men on the bus punched him, saying, "We got rules here, *Señor*. If you can't *keep'um, get outa Miami.*"

"Patti and Maritza, *tengan cuidado* (be careful)," he says. "I hate to tell you that in Florida some people don't like new people and don't like colored people. This feeling is deep. Take a look at the stores and the restaurants. Black people and white people have to use different bathrooms, get their food at different counters, and stand on separate lines. Our family is all colors—what line are *we* supposed to stand on, *carajo* (dammit)!" I didn't really understand what he meant that day.

My mother registered me for second grade in our neighborhood's Bay Ridge Elementary School. I was scared when we went to meet the principal and even more nervous when she was sort of mean to *Mami*. She kept saying: "I don't understand what you are saying, *M'am*. Could you speak more clearly?"

Mami knew all her English and she spoke it well, but sometimes the sound of it came out a little like Spanish.

"How well does Maria Stelladora speak English?" the principal asked.

On the first day of school, I felt right away that the teacher didn't like me. When the bathroom break came, the teacher told me to always use the toilet in the last stall. I could wash my hands in the janitor sink against the far wall. And speaking of hands, no one held mine when the class walked in partners to the auditorium, or to lunch, or to play in the yard. I was really lonely and felt like I didn't belong. A feeling was born in me in that school that something was wrong with me. It stayed with me for a long time.

One morning, I left my house for school just like every day. Our little house was right across a small street. I was proud that all I had to do was cross over and I was there. My mother watched me from our front yard. But on this day, the street was totally covered with tar. I looked all the way to the left, then all the way to the right. It was black, gooey, sticky tar for blocks and blocks. I started to cry. I couldn't get across and would be late for the bell. My Mom said the only way was to cross through the tar. She would throw a clean pair of shoes over to me when I got to the other side—it was a narrow road. So I crossed, and my sneakers squished down into the black stuff—the goo was even warm from the heat. And the clean shoes my mother threw over to me? They landed in the middle of the tarred road, far away from the clean school sidewalk where I was standing now.

I forced myself not to cry. I stuck out my chin, squeezed in my stomach, and wouldn't look down at my feet as I walked forward through the school lobby, up the stairs, down the second-floor hallway, and into my classroom. I finally sat down at my desk in the back of the room.

About a half hour later, when we were learning about the silent "e" at the end of words, the principal Mrs. Keeler and a man huff into our classroom. They're very upset and looking down at the tile floor—their heads follow a path up to the row where I'm sitting. They stop right at my desk.

"Here's the one," they say. "Here's the child spreading dirt all over our school. And look at the floor under her desk! Filthy, filthy, smeared with it! How dare you track your black dirt into school?"

The two monster grownups yanked me out of my seat and held me up by each of my arms. They carried me out so that my feet didn't touch their floor.

I don't remember too much more about that day. I know I waited alone in the principal's office for a long time until my mother came to get me. My family refused to send me back there. I think there were a lot of angry grownup meetings between them and the school. I never asked about it. My mother tutored me at home for a few weeks until, lucky for me, our entire family had actually, already been making plans to move to a new neighborhood. And we did that the following month.

Mom was nervous for me when we registered at my new Sandy Bluff Elementary School. Nothing too terrible happened, but still no one talked to me. Except, I was put at a classroom table with a girl named Opal. She was deaf and didn't speak very much, but she became my partner and was nice to me. Opal held my hand when we were in line. She smelled like sweet milk.

At the end of the school year, the whole class took part in a play. Mom was really happy when she heard I'd be showing off my singing and tap-dancing with a solo part. On the night of the show, she dressed me in my costume—a long red dress, white apron, and shiny black tap shoes. My teacher would do my makeup and hair at school just before the show. Excited about my big part, the family waited for me to appear onstage. When I did, this is what they saw: their seven-year-old in a red dress, white apron, black tap shoes, full head-wig of tiny, ribboned braids—and face-arms-hands-neck covered with black shoe polish. My mouth stood out with a great big smile painted in white.

And this is what they heard:
I'm a little nigger[1] doll, boo hoo, boo hoo
I ain't got no friends at all, boo hoo, boo hoo
I'm just like Topsy[2], I just growed,
Ain't got no friends I ever knowed.
Would someone come and love me so?
Boo hoo, boo hoo.

I mixed the boo hoos with loud, hard tap moves. Then finally a few "shuffle off to Buffaloes[3]" carried me off the stage.

There were many arguments in our family after that. My mother had her giant explosion. "Miami is not a good place for us. I'm leaving and moving back to New York with Maritza." I had never heard my mother to be so strong and angry when she said things to our family like: "I'm raising my daughter, not you. Miami is a pit, a hateful pit!

---

[1] An extremely derogatory racial slur used for African American and dark-skinned people, especially in the US

[2] A character from Harriet Beecher Stowe's *Uncle Tom's Cabin* (1852). The image is a nineteenth century, American stereotype of black, uneducated slave children.

[3] A dance step in choreographed American tap, which usually moves a dancer across the stage.

We have never been treated this way – dressing Maritza like a poor slave – this is how these southern *blancos* (white people) see her and all of us—uneducated and worthless! Don't kid yourself, Rose, you too. Why do you think it's taken so long for you to make broker in your company? Do you really think those American men at your real estate office, want a brown, Caribbean woman for their partner?"

So *Mami* announced, "We're leaving."

In four weeks, over many tears and family arguments, Mom packed all of our things. There were a lot of sad and mad feelings now between *Mami* and our family. I still didn't really understand what was so bad about Miami—it was just school that was bad. I could get used to it. Everything and everybody else made me happy. I cried all the way to the airport and wouldn't let go of my aunt Rose and Uncle Jorge. I didn't even want to look at my mother. I cried on the airplane ride. I was still crying when we got to New York. I thought my life was over.

Maritza
27
The Doll House
New York City, 1954–1958

It was the middle of the night when we got to LaGuardia Airport in New York City. By this time, *Mami* was sick and tired of me whining that I didn't want to leave my family in Miami.

"I'm your family, baby. We're a team, and we'll go back and visit them a lot."

Mami was exhausted. She was dragging all of our luggage because we couldn't find anyone to help us so late at night. I knew she was scared too because her lips were closed tight and she had those purple circles under her eyes. I figured I should better shut up and help her with a suitcase.

We finally got into a taxi with our things, and I fell sound asleep as soon as I saw us crossing the Triboro Bridge. When *Mami* poked me awake at the end of the ride, I saw that we were in the same neighborhood, no, the same block where we used to live a long time ago before Miami: Broadway and 165th. Street. The taxi driver helped us get the luggage into the building elevator and we went to the fifth floor. I realized that this was Elsa's house,

Mami's old friend who has a really big apartment. *Mami* had the key and we opened the door. There was a long hallway. We were staying in the first bedroom on the left. Was this like a hotel? We needed to be quiet because Elsa's family was sleeping, but I banged the suitcases on purpose anyway. I hated it.

When we opened the door to our room, it was filled with boxes and boxes of all our stuff from the little blue Miami house. Mom mailed it all to New York ahead of us.

"Where's our bed? I hate it here. I have to go to the bathroom."

Mami looked like she was almost going to cry. She washed me as best she could in the strange bathroom and put me to bed. The great big bed was in the corner of the room, and I was surrounded by tall brown boxes everywhere. I dreamed I was a prisoner in a stone tower.

When I finally woke up the next day it was almost afternoon, and I saw Mom being busy in our room, taking out our things from the suitcases. She'd pushed all the boxes to one wall so there was a lot more room. And I heard her humming in her way that said she was going to have a good day.

"Good morning, sleepyhead. Maritza, it's going to be a day of surprises, you'll see. You're going to stay with Elsa, while I do some important things for us."

"What? Stay with Elsa? I don't know Elsa anymore. She's a stranger. Some surprise!"

I started scrunching up my face for a long whine, when Elsa, the stranger, appeared holding a pink tray with a toasted ham and cheese sandwich, potato chips and cocoa.

"It's okay, *Mami*. I'll stay with Elsa."

Before she left, *Mami* explained that Elsa was a friend of our family. She was letting us stay in her house for a few weeks until we got settled in New York. "Be polite to this lady, and don't make any messes in her house, okay?"

The afternoon with Elsa was very long, and there was nowhere I could get out. The front door of that big apartment just led out to a hall with other apartment doors, and an elevator door with numbers that lit up on top. I fiddled with Elsa's door locks and got them open. Like a dodo, I just stood there watching the elevator numbers flash and listening to the motor noise when the elevator went up and down. I said to no one, "Hello, hello, hello." I got a little echo from the hallway.

Elsa caught me. "What are you doing, little girl? Never, ever open my door or leave the apartment without your mother. You got it?"

She spit when she talked. Hmph. I'm going to tell my mother she yelled at me.

I know Elsa has a big son named Willy. Which room was his? I quietly tiptoed down the hall and opened the door across from our room. Oh, this was definitely his room. There was a blue plaid spread on his wooden bed and a pair of boy sneakers – those high ones – on the floor. But the best part of the room was the ceiling. It had all kinds of airplanes, wooden ones and paper ones, hanging from strings! Did he make them? The window was like ours, but in front of Willy's window was a funny tilted desk covered with all sorts of drawings. I didn't touch anything. Was Willy a boy or a man? When was he coming home, so I could see him? As I left Willy's room, Elsa said, "Maritza, what are you doing? Do you want to watch TV with me?"

"No, thank you, Elsa. I'm going to take a nap."

It was around the afternoon when I woke up, and *Mami* was home. She had on a smile that was almost like her real one.

"Guess what, baby? I think they're going to accept you at the All Souls Grammar School. Tomorrow we'll go for you to see it and meet the principal. If you like it, that'll be your new school, okay?"

I was shaking a little when I visited the school the next day. I liked the girls in their maroon plaid uniform jumpers and white, white blouses. I could be like them. Even though I thought I was happy when we went to measure me for my new uniforms, then I wasn't sure. It was really *Mami* who kept telling me that I felt this way. I was kind of mixed up.

After settling my school, Mom's next big job was as she said, "Finding us a beautiful place to live." One day, after apartment hunting all afternoon, she came back looking really down and tired.

"Maritza, the only lucky thing that happened to me today is in this bag. I didn't find any apartments, too expensive; but the pet store was giving away goldfish for free if you bought a bowl. I thought these would be fun for you."

Out of the big bag she took out a glass bowl, a little can of fish food, and a clear container where two fish were swimming around. One was a real goldfish, and the other one was brown with big googly eyes that popped out. I loved them! When we set them up with water and food, I put them on our windowsill.

Time for bed. Was it a good day? I don't know. All I knew is that it felt so different without my family. I was afraid about my mother being afraid, about our new life not beginning until we got out of this room. Were we going to stay prisoners here forever? I thought about these things as I went to sleep. In the morning, my mother told me two things: that I cried out in the night and that both fish died. The goldfish had jumped out of the bowl and out of the open window. The googly one was floating dead at the top of the bowl. "*Mami,* do you see? Even the fish have to get out of here!"

Boring days passed at Elsa's. I couldn't wait to start school in two weeks. Keeping each other company in her ugly kitchen, Elsa showed me how to play gin rummy and casino. But I started to beat her, and she wouldn't play with me anymore. In fact, she was grumpy with me now. What kind of grownup is that? I've read all the books *Mami* brought home for me, and I did jacks, pick up sticks and Candyland with myself. Really boring.

Now this week, Mom started to come home from her apartment hunting with a real, not a fake, smile on her face.

I even heard her singing. I couldn't believe it. She even looked nicer, like with earrings and pretty blouses. "*Mami*, what is it? Are you happy? About what? About what?"

Finally, she said, "Well, maybe, I found a nice, new apartment for us."

"Really, where?"

"Well, it's a very special building a little further uptown, right off Broadway and only a few blocks from your school. It's a brownstone with only one other family living there, who are the owners. And, there is such a big surprise in this building that you're never going to believe it!"

"What?"

"I'm not going to tell you, so when you discover it, you'll be *en las nuves* (on cloud nine). You'll find out the day we move in. If I can get everything ready, we'll move next weekend. Don't tell Elsa, I'll handle that."

"Sure Mom. Elsa's been in a bad mood with me lately. I don't like her."

"Neither do I, it's time to get the *hecky* out of here."

"Hmph, you said it."

Just like she promised, Mom and I moved the next weekend. I can't remember the last time I saw her so excited. She even started acting a little silly. So, when we got into Elsa's elevator for the last time, we both stuck out our tongues at her apartment door and then laughed like crazy. I carried my fishbowl for when I got new goldfish soon who would stay alive this time. Mom carried a leather case with her important papers, money, and her picture of

Jesus inside. Everything else had been packed and delivered to the new apartment. As a treat, we took a yellow checker taxi to the new house. Before getting there, Mom told the driver to take a slow ride around our new neighborhood. There was my new school on Wadsworth Ave. All Souls Grammar, with the beautiful church right next door. Then, five blocks away, our new house. It was on a pretty block with a row of brownstones, like dollhouses, that all looked alike to me.

"How do we find ours?"

Each house had stone steps leading to a glass main door: ours said 657 at the top of the door.

Mom opened the door with her new key. It was quiet and still inside. The front hall had a round rug in the middle and a shiny brass lamp hanging from the middle of the ceiling. We started up the staircase to the fourth floor. The first three floors belonged to the owner's family; the fourth floor was ours.

"Wait Mom, did I hear kids giggling?"

"Oh, that's just the creaky stairs," said Mom.

But as we passed the third floor, I definitely heard a door slam and more giggles. "Hey, what's going on around here?" I was really curious, but now we were almost on the fourth floor. It was the top floor with sunshine all over. Right over our apartment door, Number #2, was a window in the ceiling, and the light and sky were coming in. It was almost like Miami light. Mom said you call this kind of window a skylight. We go inside and the same sunshine is in the living room.

"Wow!" It's all fixed up like our real home: all our own comfy furniture, our TV, the coffee table with the little lion's feet, and even curtains on the window. There's a fireplace with pink tiles that Mom said was definitely big enough for Santa. And down the hall was a big kitchen with our dining room furniture, already covered with a tablecloth.

"*Mami,* I love it, this is our real house? When did you do this?"

Mom was happy, I was happy. "I did a little bit every day," she said. "All those boring afternoons when you stayed with Elsa."

Beyond the living room was the miracle. In the bedroom were two beautiful, pink, Hollywood twin beds, with curved tops and little gold buttons. I always wanted a Hollywood bed. The windows had white lacy curtains— you know, the ones you can kind of see through, but make things all fuzzy outside…

All of a sudden, there was knocking on our front door, and I ran to open it, before even asking who it was. Standing in front of me were the two cutest little girls I'd ever seen.

"Hi, we live in this house," they say. "*Wanna* play?" They look like twins. They had curly Tony perms and their hair was parted to the side with bow barrettes. They were wearing the same outfit. "We have on our Spanish *señorita* costumes: you see the curly ruffles on the skirt? Our Mom lets us wear them on special days. It was us laughing when you were coming up the stairs."

Everyone was laughing now, even *Mami* who came over to the door. She said, "So darling, do you like the surprise? These little girls live right here, right downstairs. Margie and Mary Murillo. They're Cuban, like your father. Their parents own the whole building and they're our friends…"

I didn't wait to hear what else she said because the girls were pulling me out of the apartment, whispering, "We'll show you all our special places and secrets." And we were gone.

Besides loving living above the Murillos in the dollhouse, I was learning some things about how other people and families behaved. Not all mothers made their children's clothes or were with them all the time, watching, watching, watching. Mothers could love other people besides their children, like their husbands. And kids didn't have to make sure their mothers were feeling happy. They just played and did kid things without checking if their mother was okay. Margie and Mary cared about getting into trouble; I cared about hurting my mother's feelings.

The Mom, Lorena, was different from anyone I had ever met. Lorena was a bit of an older lady. She had wrinkles on her face and walked like her feet hurt. Lots of eye makeup too. She didn't wear "mom" clothes like *Mami* or my aunts. She wore long loose gowns with bright colors, beads around her neck and big rings on her fingers. Sometimes she wore a turban, and most of the time, her nails were blood red. She was nice, but not huggy with her children like my Mom was. When Margie and Mary were naughty, they always got a swat. I got sent to my room, with a talk.

The sisters loved to find their parents' secrets, like rolls of money in the bureau drawers or chocolates in the freezer. One day, after days of planning for when their mother Lorena would be out shopping, the girls brought me into their mother's special room on the second floor of the house. It was the biggest secret ever. They told me their mother was a kind of priest, called a *santera.* She was like a holy person who had magic.

"People come to ask her for cures and spells," said Margie.

"What's a spell?"

"It's making someone do what you want, change their mind. Like, make them love you. This room is where people come to see *Mama Lorena.* If she ever catches us in here, we're dead, but let's look around anyway."

Margie was definitely the brave one. I was really scared.

The special room smelled like a church, with incense burning in a little gold pot. One wall was made of glass cubes that let in pretty light from the hanging lamp in the front hall. Statues were everywhere on little altars with fresh flowers. Some statues had beads around them with bowls of shiny pennies at their feet. I recognized a Jesus statue and a saint, Mary said, was St. Lazarus. He was standing on crutches as if he was hurt, and his face and arms were bloody. I didn't really understand what Mary explained, but it was something like, "This saint man feels people's pain, and when you sing and pray to him, your pain goes away."

"Who sings to him?" I asked.

"That's what our *Mami* does, silly. I told you she was a priest! And sometimes she washes the people's feet who come to see her. She puts perfume in the water, and she cures them." Mary looked so proud of her Mom.

"Wow," I mumbled. I was terrified. I never heard of anything like this in my life. I said we should go.

After a few months of living in the dollhouse, something else happened on the second floor where Lorena did her magic: my mother started a business in Lorena's parlor. This was the other special room on that floor of the brownstone. No, no, *Mami* didn't become a *santera*, holy person. She became a private teacher who taught English to people from Spanish-speaking countries or to American people who wanted to learn proper Spanish. Her first student was Lorena herself, who learned fast and thought Mom was the greatest.

She said, "Patti, I know you're looking for a job. Why don't you just start your own business, teaching here in my parlor? Just pay me a little rent, and we'll both be happy!" Mom got a little annoyed though, when Lorena wouldn't let her hang her Teacher's College diploma on the parlor wall.

So, Mom started a teaching business in the dollhouse. I think it's going to become her real job.

Maritza
28
Eyes Wide Open
New York City, Miami, Late 1950s

I convinced myself that Margie and Mary were my real blood cousins from Cuba, on my father's side. We were inseparable, including being out on the street riding bikes and skating. "Stay on our block only," said the mothers. But we didn't. This was the closest I had come to having siblings and I was having a ball!

There were other kids too, like my classmate from All Souls, Barbara Murphy, who lived right across the street and we visited each other's houses. The Murphy's house was so different from mine. Everything was quiet because there was a sick grandma there. And, one time I couldn't believe it, I saw a priest watching TV in their living room.

"What is a priest, a Catholic priest, doing in your house?"

"He's my Uncle Bill, he's visiting," said Barbara.

I had never seen a priest in a real house before, doing real human things. *Mama Lorena* didn't count, I was used to her.

School was my heaven. It was a magic kingdom of maps, countries I would visit one day, the solar system, and loads more. The older I got, the more enormous this kingdom became to me. Once I saw this bigness, I began to understand how the tiny, safe world *Mami* had created for us was definitely not the whole world. I saw how Mom worked to keep me inside with her. Her world was kindness, puppet shows, visiting sick friends on Sunday, the holy day, proper manners, no outbursts, smiling politeness to adults and dancing lessons of every kind. She would never think of a job in the outside world where I'd have to stay with a babysitter. Instead, she worked long hours teaching her students in the parlor and handing out her business cards to people who needed to learn English. I understood how this guaranteed that she would always be home with me. She was the guard against the influence of the outside world. She thought.

School was where I was practicing how to be in the big world. I think I was a bit of a show-off there: winning spelling bees and debates, and this year I became class president. And then there were all the things to understand outside of school in the real world: about people, New York City, subway routes, how the post office worked. And what was the big fuss about Raúl Galante in Puerto Rey? And why do some of my Mom's new Cuban friends say, *"Viva Fidel"?*

I discovered that the more I learned, the bigger I became in my head. I thought that my mind was actually starting to change. Now that I was ten, I was almost thinking like a grownup! Remember how I used to think like a child when I was only a baby? Well, I'll tell you just for the record, that my vocabulary now was very advanced for my age, and my main job was keeping my eyes and ears wide open so that I could learn everything.

Another thing I was working on was trying to understand why people did and didn't do things. My first subject of study, of course, was Mom herself. I saw her. I knew the "deep her" and I was upset with what I understood. I was mad at her for being a child grownup; I believed I was a grownup child. She was so cautious, she needed to keep things small and safe. Yes, yes, I know. I know she was only a baby girl when her mother died; that Aunt Rose raised her with the grumpy General; that her husband died. But couldn't she just forget all that stuff? Some of this happened to Aunt Rose too, you know. But she was so different, like an explorer. And look at me. I lost Gabriel too!

So, I've been giving Mom some maturity ideas.

"Mom, let's move to a bigger apartment."

"*Mami,* why don't you teach *kids* in your home school, not just grownups? You know, some Cuban families are in our neighborhood now, and their kids at my school can't speak English. Why don't you teach them?"

"Mom, can I call the telephone company so we can get one of those new princess phones in pink?"

And we did do those things. Our move to a larger place in a six-story building on Ft. Washington Avenue was perfect for us. Mom grew her school in our large, new living room. The only bad thing was leaving Margie and Mary, my soul sisters. We cried on moving day like it was the end of the world, but they would be inside me forever. They taught me how to have as much fun as I could being a kid: that was my job. Sometimes it got me into trouble, and sometimes it scared my mother, but so what? I had to do it.

It was a few years before Mom and I returned to Miami after our big exit. Rose and Jorge visited us in New York, but Mom didn't want us to go to Miami until her teaching business was successful enough to buy us a real vacation. She had to show her bossy sister she could take care of her little family herself. Pretty soon *Mami* became so busy she was teaching all the time. Grownups in the morning while I was in school. Then the big rush of kids at four p.m., who came for after-school tutoring. Sometimes she even had grownups at night. While I knew the home school was my mother's business, as I got older, I resented coming home in the afternoons to bridge tables and chairs all over our living room, and squirming kids speaking terrible English. *Mami* said that my great report cards were the best advertisement for her home school. Mothers would stop me and ask, "Are you Doña Patti's daughter, the lady who is the tutor? Tell her I want to speak to her about my child." Sometimes I wouldn't give the message.

When we started visiting Miami again, we discovered a big change. Rose and Jorge were the busiest people I'd ever seen. The first surprise was that the little blue house where Mom and I had lived was knocked down. The empty lot was filled with workers, including Uncle Jorge, constructing an eight-unit apartment building.

"Who's going to live there?" I asked Rose.

"Renters, of course, who are going to pay us month after month forever! Doesn't that sound great? And we're going to do this all over Miami by building more apartment buildings."

Yes, she did do this eventually, but that was after she bought two beauty salons and opened a real estate company that sold hundreds of homes to Cuban families just arriving in Miami during the Cuban revolution. I know this because Mom worked as a bookkeeper for the Gavilán-Gordon Realty (Rose Gavilán was the principal broker, of course) for all the years we spent our summers in that tropical Miami sun.

I still loved Miami—it was the first place I ever felt free from Mom. As soon as we arrived at the Miami airport, the soil, flowers and humid smell gave me a heavenly feeling. But I was older now, so running barefoot and picking mangoes with Pammy now changed to visiting Rose's business office. Off went the sneakers and shorts and on came a nice dress and shoes. *Tía* took me everywhere. Sometimes to the bank, sometimes to show a fancy house. I was in another kind of heaven. I watched my Aunt Rose do business in the big world. I thought she was a big shot: she acted like one.

"This is how you get a property loan, Maritza." She sat me down and explained what a mortgage was. "It's also how you settle a construction contract and get the best price on a new blue Mercury with air-conditioning. I do all of this while still being a charming and refined Latin lady. Watch closely, because these are *your* young lady lessons. In North America, we keep our morals, and work hard for everything we want!"

"*Sí, Tía,* yes Auntie." I had no idea what she was talking about—it was just fun.

One Saturday morning Aunt Rose said, "Maritza, tonight I'm really going to show you something important." We arrived, dressed up, at a fancy hotel dinner that was only for ladies. My aunt had been accepted into the *Miami Chapter of the National Business and Professional Women's Association.* During dinner, she pointed out several ladies.

"You see that small woman over there wearing the green dress? She's a judge. You see the blond lady sitting at the end of our table? She's a doctor. I'm a businesswoman, that makes me like all of them."

My *Tía,* our family's Rosina Dorada was becoming someone new. She was someone I wanted to be with as much as I could. What would Mom think?

So much happened during my summers in Miami, experiences that kept my eyes open all the time. We did important business things and family things. Every single Sunday afternoon, we drove the cool '57 Mercury for three hours to visit Aunt Nina. She was still very mentally ill and lived at the Del Rey State Psychiatric Hospital just outside of Miami. *Tía, Tío, Mami* and I packed into the car with casseroles of the Caribbean home food Nina loved. The hospital was a strange place—not good, not bad. It was on many perfect acres of green grass and tall palm trees. Scattered all over were two-story perfectly white buildings, where the patients lived. There were buildings for the men, buildings for the ladies and houses for children with swings outside. There were houses for patients who were just coming into the hospital and even a building for patients who were soon going home. My Nina was in the ladies' unit where I didn't see a single man, not even a male doctor.

"Maritza," said Rose sternly. "Stay close to us in the hospital. No wandering around by yourself the way you do. Some people who live here are a little unpredictable."

"What does that mean?"

"Crazy!" said my mother.

"Now stop it, Patti," said *Tía*. "What are you, a child?"

I knew *Mami* hated coming to the hospital. She loved her sister Nina and had spent so many years protecting her and being like her twin. But now, my mother was afraid of Nina's sickness, as well as the psychiatric hospital where she lived. Her little sister had become a frightening stranger to her. I didn't like this part of my mother. It made me sad.

The front desk nurse led us down a hall to a large room called the "Day Room." Family children like me were allowed to come too. This is where the patients who were a little better, spent their day.

"I'll get Miss Nina," said the nurse in a soft voice "She's been dressed and waiting for you since breakfast."

We all sat on an empty sofa, across from a lady I said hi to. The woman was a little different, but I tried not to be scared because I had seen her a lot of times before on our visits. Bald spots were all over her head, and the rest of her hair was very short like a man's. She had no front teeth. Could she speak? I'd never heard her. I wondered, did she have a family like us? Aunt Nina suddenly floated into the room looking like my duchess. She was a pale angel with red lipstick.

The bald-spotted lady stood up and said politely, "Your family is here, Nina. Why don't you take my seat so you can all be together?" And she walked away with a little wiggle. You can be sick in your mind and still have a kind heart. That's what I learned.

As always, my best listening place in Miami was the step outside Aunt Rose's porch. I heard a lot that I needed to keep in my mind. Nina's illness, they said, was called paranoid schizophrenia. She wouldn't get much better unless she could take a special new medicine they were just inventing. It was called Thorazank or Thorazine, I think. How do we get that for her, I wondered? And then there was talk and sometimes crying about bad things in Puerto Rey. I heard the grownups become really upset about my Uncle Victor and his family in the capital city. "Dangerous," *peligroso,* they said. There was something about *niñas* disappearing. What? How could girls disappear? Mom never let me out of her sight! I asked about this and was told to stay away from talk that wasn't for children. But I couldn't help listening from some other hiding place.

At the gatherings in *Tía* and *Tío's* house, more people visited and sometimes gave speeches. Our handsome cousins, Bobby and José (the sons of Zoraya and Nino, who helped Rose get to America) talked about Puerto Reyan politics and asked for donations—that meant giving money because you believed in something. I didn't know exactly what the money was for, except it had to do with freeing their country, Puerto Rey, and stopping the awful things that were happening to people there.

Bobby came over alone one evening to see Uncle Jorge. They talked in the dining room while Rose made them a *cafecito*. When she carried the coffee in, she stopped suddenly and in a low, but very strong voice told Bobby to leave. She didn't let him explain.

"Out," she said. Rose turned to Uncle Jorge and in the same stern voice said, "If you agree to drive Bobby's truck to the Miami airport for that group of *locos* (crazy people) who think they're soldiers, don't bother coming back home."

I found out from Rose and Jorge's all-night argument that Bobby, Jose and a group of about twelve men were going to fly a plane from Miami to Catalina, Puerto Rey, to overthrow President Galante. They needed a driver to deliver their secret plane cargo to the Miami airfield. But two weeks later, from my hiding place under the front porch, I heard it. Our cousins' project was a total disaster. José, the younger boy, was literally torn apart by Galante's soldiers and died. Bobby returned a changed person. Their mother, Zoraya, never recovered from losing her sons. I was really scared by what I heard. Maybe keeping my eyes and ears wide open wasn't such a good idea. After all, I was only a child.

Maritza
29
Tío
New York City; Late 1950s

My Uncle Victor – the youngest brother of *Mami*, Rose and Nina, aka baby Victor, foster son of the American mistresses, Methodist minister, certified accountant for the Puerto Reyan government, husband and father of four children – is in big trouble. I think he is doing something very good and very bad in his country. This is the only way I can understand this right now.

Last week, *Mami* received a letter from Uncle Victor's wife, Julia, saying that Victor was coming to New York in two weeks. "He's going to beg the United States for permission to move us all there." Julia told *Mami* she was scared. She said that at dinner Victor gave long talks about "personal sacrifice" and "doing the right thing." Julia wrote: "It's as if he's preparing us for something. The children don't understand him but feel that something is going on with their *Papá*. Last night, he put on his minister voice, like he was on the pulpit at Church, and said:

Children, sometimes life asks us to do the most challenging things. God will have us put what we most love at risk. We must be ready to sacrifice the personal comforts of our family and home if there is a greater good to be achieved. God chooses some of us for this. The island nation of Puerto Rey, which your ancestors helped to build, is now a pit of brutality, injustice and ungodliness. The rights of our people are gone when someone can be dragged out of his house and not seen again. There is a possibility I could be taken. I would no longer be able to be your loving father. You will eventually learn to take comfort in the fact that your loss will have hopefully contributed toward the freedom of our country.

My Mom tells me simply that my Uncle Victor will be visiting us in two weeks, and that I'll have a little chance to get to know him. *Mami* has no idea I've read the letter from Aunt Julia, or that I have any knowledge of the troubles in Puerto Rey. Doesn't she notice that I know things?

It was a chilly spring day when he arrived. I got home from school and Mom says *Tío* Victor has been with her since that morning. "He's taking a walk now, just waiting for you to come home." My coat and hat were still on when I heard the front door of our apartment open, and into the living room walked a tall man wearing a long overcoat and brimmed hat. I couldn't make out his face because of the sun coming in behind him from the living room windows. There were no thoughts in my mind. My legs just ran to him, and I squeezed him so hard, as if I had known him all my life. I had. I think my whole self was expecting the father in the picture who was holding me as a baby. As I hugged him, I smelled his smell. My ear was up against his silver tie-clasp and it felt a little cold. The spell was broken by the deep voice in *Tío's* chest. "Maritza, Maritza, at last!" he said in perfect English.

He held me out and we looked at each other's smiling faces. Victor was *café con leche* color (coffee with milk color) like my mother, with very short curly hair and small, bright, twinkly eyes like my whole family. My uncle smiled, but he didn't laugh. That said something about him, but I didn't know what yet. Over dinner, *Tío* acted like a nice parent at the table, including me in all the conversation about every one of his four children: Victor Jr., Harry, Ronny and Anita, my favorite because she was a girl cousin. Uncle Victor told us he would like to move to New York to be closer to us, his family.

Mami surprised me the next day when she said I could take a little break off from school to spend the whole day with my uncle, just the two of us. I couldn't believe it. I wore a nice dress and my royal blue Sunday coat. On the long bus ride down Broadway and Riverside Drive, my shyness flew out the bus window.

"Let's both be New York tourists," he said. We stopped at the giant Riverside Church, where the wind from the Hudson River practically knocked us over. Then General Grant's tomb, and I told my uncle about the Civil War and General Grant's victory, in case he didn't know. After cheeseburgers at White Castle – *Tío* had two, I had one – we walked toward Central Park. My Uncle Victor still didn't laugh, but I felt good with him. Mostly quiet, we walked all the way across Sheep's Meadow toward the carousel. The sun was shining, and I held his big hand the whole time.

Three happy rides on the up-and-down horses with crazy music, and we were both exhausted and deaf. As we headed for home on the uptown bus, *Tío* told me again that he was trying very, very hard to move to the United States with his family.

"Tomorrow, I have appointments at the United Nations and the U.S. Immigration Office to ask if I can move as soon as possible. "No, Maritza, you can't come with me... And yes, I do like my country, but I don't want to live there anymore. Listen to me now, you should know this: Tomorrow night I'm going to Washington, D.C., to ask for permission, some more."

I mumbled something like, "I can't wait till you come, *Tío*," and fell sound asleep on his shoulder after he gently undid the top button of my coat. I only saw Uncle Victor one more time—from my living room window the next day when Mom and I waved goodbye to him in his airport taxi. Mom told me that after one day in Washington, *Tío* would go back home to his family in Puerto Rey. "By God's grace, we'll see him again soon."

In the time Uncle Victor waited in his country for asylum permission to the United States, he got his family ready. I looked up what asylum means: it's when a safe country like the U.S., lets you come to live there because your own country can hurt you. During the time *Tío* waited, I overheard from grownups who visited my house that two of Victor's friends had been hurt, tortured in jail and now *están muertos* (they are dead). Torture means when someone hurts you on purpose over and over again until you die or almost die. Then I heard that *Tío's* neighbors next door, Señor and Señora Peña, never came home from work one day. Their children waited home alone for them all night.

Six weeks after his visit to us, my Uncle Victor was murdered by the Puerto Reyan secret police, just a few miles from his home. He was shot in the head at close range. His wife Julia and my cousins Victor Jr., Harry, Ronny and Anita were wounded too but didn't die. I learned all this as I tried to fall asleep in my bedroom and my mother cried in the kitchen with our family and friends, far into the night. During the day, *Mami* was mostly silent and would not tell me anything. My heart was breaking—another father, gone.

I felt there was real danger in our lives now—Mom acted in some strange ways she never fully explained. She began to pick me up at school. Can you believe that? What middle schooler wants their mother waiting on the school corner? Mornings were fine for walking to school with friends, but the big "but" was how to walk the sidewalk: "Don't walk on the street too close to the buildings because someone could snatch you, drag you inside, and take you to the roof and kill you. Don't walk too close to parked cars. Someone could tempt you inside, and you'll never be seen again. Always walk in the middle of the street. And stay with your friends!"

Home became scary too. I wasn't supposed to answer the phone. Sometimes the phone would ring over, and over again and when Mom answered it, no one was there. She was really upset, and I got the feeling she believed someone bad was calling. Aunt Rose complained that funny things were happening around her house in Florida too: twice she found a stranger in her backyard looking around.

"Patti, be very careful," said Rose. "You never know how far that dictator's arm can reach. There's a reason they call him *el Pulpo*, the Octopus.

One night, I screamed, "What the heck is going on, *Mami*? Why are you acting so strange? I'm scared. At night, why do you keep our coats and street shoes at the foot of your bed, instead of our bathrobes?"

"In case there's a fire," she said in a way that told me not to ask any more.

Being the student of my mother that I was, I figured out that her strange ideas had to do with my Uncle Victor's death. This was the whispered conversation, the terrible thing, the reason for the fear that was now part of our everyday lives. But it took me until age thirteen to finally find out all the details of his death and what happened to his family. It was still happening to his family because my Aunt Julia and my four beautiful, unknown cousins were living in hiding in a different country that protected them so they wouldn't be murdered too.

From talk in the night kitchen, I learned, "The children were kidnapped after… " From whispering on the telephone, I heard something like, "There was no face... shot at close range... " And from the porch steps on a Miami visit, I heard someone scream, *"¡Ayá no se puede vivir, no se puede vivir! ¡Es una sentencia de muerte!"* (You can't live, you can't live there! It's a death sentence to be there!) I heard those screams when I was thirteen and finally went to my Aunt Rose to ask for the whole story of my Uncle Victor's death. She told me with no expression on her face, without taking a single breath, it seemed to me:

Your Tío Victor was a finance administrator for the Puerto Reyan government in the division of Commercial Trade. It was his living, apart from being a Minister. He was a well-respected employee there. But most importantly, he was an underground worker in the effort to overthrow the Galante government—the horrible dictatorship in our country that permitted itself to kill people, rob their businesses, and jail them if they complained. Your uncle was in a secret group. Together, in Victor's subcellar, they printed information and newspapers about the truths of the dictatorship. One day in July, Victor received an emergency telephone signal – three rings three times – the secret police was on its way. Your uncle, your Aunt Julia, and another colleague who was working with Victor rushed out of the house in their Pontiac to pick up each of the four children at their four different schools. This was done for protection, so on a day like this day, the secret police couldn't find them all at once.

When the children were gathered, the car headed for the Italian embassy where Victor knew he could get refuge. As they reached the embassy gate, a secret police car screeched to a stop between Victor's car and the gate. Agents with guns spilled out and screamed at your uncle as he stepped out of his Pontiac. Victor said some ridiculous things in the name of God, as an agent from only one meter away, shot him on the right side of his face. Victor Jr., at sixteen years old, jumped out of the car to protect his father and was hit in the stomach even before he was fully standing. The rest of the men opened fire on the Pontiac. Your Aunt Julia was shot as she laid over the rest of the children on the car floor.

Aunt Rose had turned pale. "*El descaro*—the disgrace," she said. "is that in about fifteen minutes, the embassy entrance, the street, the onlookers were gone, because cars came and took the family away to unknown places. And your Uncle Victor? A pickup truck came and dumped his body in the back as if he were a sack of rice."

"That's all I'll tell you now, Maritza. It's enough for now, darling. You're so young to know these things. Your mother is like a child herself, as if it is her mother, as if it is her husband, Gabriel, dying all over again. You have to forgive these tender parts of her. That's why you have me. The last thing you should know now is that your Aunt Julia and your cousins are safe, in a country that is protecting them… No, I can't tell you where."

Maritza
30
No Hablo Español
New York City, 1958–1962

I changed after all this. I knew that your family could die; that mothers could hold you prisoner; and that loving aunts could develop disturbed minds. I also knew that I could feel small in the outside world just because my family was from the Caribbean. The nuns called me "the smart Spanish girl" at school. This meant they expected kids from immigrant families like mine to be stupid. It was kind of like when they dressed me up like Topsy in Miami, only a little nicer. What kind of a world was that? It sure wasn't one Mom was willing to explain or protect me from.

Outside of understanding these things, I wanted no further information from Mom at this time. I just needed to think on my own and watch the world very carefully, then I could figure out what I wanted to do in it. I invented a brilliant plan to keep out my mother's useless noise. I swindeled her by being present, but not really being with her. I stopped speaking Spanish—the language of our personal world. ¡*No hablo español*! What a cut this was! Brilliant meanness. I knew that. She said something to me in Spanish. I just answered her in English. I rocked her with my ever-enriched high school prep vocabulary, so she was never totally sure what I was talking about. We were two universes passing in the night, and that was exactly the way I wanted it. If I could take a break from the Spanish that expressed the love and sadness in our lives, maybe I could focus on the worldly things I wanted: to be an American girl. I wasn't totally leaving Mom. I knew I loved her. But I didn't want to need her right now. Without realizing it, Mom kind of confirmed this new juncture in our relationship. When I got my first menstruation, she actually said, "Now what are we going to do with you?" As if girls with periods were no longer part of her skill set.

At thirteen, cutting my Spanish was only the beginning. To grow me, I made myself the child of whatever influence taught me something I wanted to know. Thank goodness I was sensible. In my last year at All Souls School, 8th grade, I heard a story that roly-poly Sister Angela, our school principal, ran a business before she became a nun. One day when she had patrol duty in the cafeteria, I went up to her and asked, "How do you know what foods to buy for all the kids in our school?"

"That's a good question, girlie. Don't tell anybody, but I buy the things I like to eat—like mac and cheese."

So, we giggled together, and she asked me if I'd like to help her after school, filling out the food orders. I got a job! On Tuesdays, I took her scribbled list and entered the foods she wanted on a big form. Two cases of baked beans, check. One case of powdered mashed potatoes, check. Ten pounds of frankfurter links, okay. And on and on I went. At thirteen, I became her office assistant.

During this time I also spent many afternoons at the homes of my classmates, who were mostly Irish girls. The O'Neills, the Donovans, the Fitzpatricks—I liked the way they were. They had straight hair, told jokes and drank tea. I knew Tap, they did Irish dancing. They had brothers and sisters and fathers; I had my Mom and my aunts and uncle. I loved their lamb chops and peas, and I wanted Mom to cook plain like they did, without garlic and salt. So, Mom cooked this way once a week and called it our "*American* dinner night."

I began to be plainer too, with none of the bows or curls in my hair, just brushed out with what I called American bangs—except mine never layed flat, they always curled at the ends. I idolized my friend Annie McDonald's big sister, Betsy. Boy, was she smart! From graduating eighth grade at All Souls, she now went to the Blessed Saints High School for Girls, all the way downtown; so, you had to take a bus. She was gorgeous and bouncy and on the school honor roll. She looked fabulous in her crisp white blouse, and smart navy-blue blazer with gold buttons and the school insignia on the pocket. I wanted to be her. I wanted to go to that private school. I had the grades. Four of my friends already applied. Mom *had* to enroll me. I knew this was the right thing.

From the phone booth at the corner pharmacy, I started calling Aunt Rose in Miami. Mom was going to be really jealous about this. *Tía* was my hero now, ever since she told me the truth about Uncle Victor. She lived in the world I wanted to live in. My aunt knew the Blessed Saints School and said she would talk to Mom.

The following year, I was a girl in a navy-blue blazer, plaid skirt, oxfords, a beret and occasionally white gloves, who took the Number 5 bus from 168th Street to 86th Street and Riverside Drive. I was with my best friends riding to Blessed Saints, in the back of the bus, doing homework and joking about all the grumpy passengers on their way to downtown jobs. Just taking the bus to a destination without my mother was heaven.

BS, as we hilariously called it, was my place. I knew it. Small and cozy, it was perched on the top two floors of an old gothic building—and it was wide open for me. I'm \one of the A students. I'm serious, naughty and funny at the same time. This was a way of being *me* that grew. I got my class to protest daily Mass and the awful cafeteria food. I behaved in ways that were a new me – a free me – a way, far away from the cocooned me. I got weekly demerits for hiking my uniform skirt to mini length – it was the 1960s – and smoking in the Balcony Diner across the street from school. The most forbidden thing I did was start a club—a sorority, the RRR. Wild horses wouldn't ever get me to tell what that stood for, but I'll give you a hint that we got the name from MAD Magazine.

"What are we going to do with *ya,* Miss Durán?" Sister Marguerite, head of discipline and incomprehensible in her Irish brogue speaks to me calmly with pink cheeks and perspiration pouring from her bonnet. "How can you be on the dean's list, compete in the *debatin'* team, work at the Foundling with the orphans, and also be such a fresh article? It must be somethin' about your kind. You Spanish are an odd lot!"

I didn't care. I lived now in a happy, dizzy world of new friends, boys from our brother school, and learning about everything. The nucleus is the brain of the cell and photosynthesis is how plants make food: I want to be a scientist! The electoral college chooses the president: I should be the mayor of New York first! Mary Queen of Scots was beheaded by her rival. I'm going to study in England and become a history professor! Glen T. Seborg is head of the Atomic Energy Commission at the United Nations: the best thing is to be a diplomat—science and politics together! Don't you think?

Every year of high school was a march further out into what I believed was the right path for me. I was a leader at BS, always a class officer and the President of the Sodality of Mary. I got most of my friends to join, and we had a blast collecting money and buying Christmas presents for people who didn't have as much as we did. I found out that old people who were poor, really did live in dirty nursing homes that smelled like urine; and that most of the Foundling Hospital babies I played with on weekends, would never have real parents.

I haven't told you about God. I felt that he floated around me, but I could never be sure. I wanted to be inspired by the lives of the great saints. I prayed. Like every other swoony girl at my high school, I read about the saints and wanted to fall in love with them. But how could you ever be like young St. Teresa of Avila? How did she give away all her stuff? And about God, I secretly believed the way my whole family did—that you talked to God and listened to him in your own way. Not the way the Church told you to do it. Mom said all those rules about how people should be married, and the meat you're not supposed to eat on Friday... "That's just people, the priests, human beings like you and me making up those rules. Not God! You just listen, listen to the voice inside you—that's God. Then as you grow, you'll be guided about what life path to follow. You'll know it when you're in it."

I said secretly to myself, "I'm in it, Mom. I *am* on my path. I know I am."

In a shaky way, my mother managed to be happy for me because the fact was that I was just growing, for goodness' sake and not doing anything delinquent. I was moving further away from her. She knew this, but she also realized that I was having a good time. Mom was trying her best to keep up with my swallowing the entire world in front of me, but she was like someone on a roller coaster ride where death could happen at any moment. Spanish with her was still *nada*, nothing. I knew this probably hurt her, but I just couldn't risk it: she would pull me in again. She would fill me with so much Caribbean food and sad eyes, that I would never be able to grow myself. Spanish was the language of *us*\. English was just its shorthand. I knew this. I didn't want to go there.

And then, I loved boys.

Maritza
31
American
New York City, 1960s

I wasn't easy with the boy thing. I didn't get them. I was shy there. Growing up with just Mom in the house and having my sweetie, Uncle Jorge, for only weeks at a time every year had done something to me. But I tried. I wanted them to look at me, but when they did, I felt nervous, embarrassed, shy, happy—all at once. Was that nuts? Then there was another thing. Did I want to like an American one or a Latin one? In my neighborhood there were a bunch of Cuban boys who I kind of knew. Lots of people from Havana were now in New York and Miami because of the revolution in Cuba. Their parents hated Fidel Castro.

Anyway, these guys were totally handsome and I saw them at neighborhood birthday parties. Their eyes always got to me—something "come to me, baby" about them. Our mothers stopped by to chaperone and everybody got dressed up, the boys with ties, and the girls with these tight pencil skirts with slits in the back. They usually wore fitted sweaters, pink lipstick, and as high a heel as their moms would let them wear. They all looked like this, except for me. It was the sixties. For me, it was a mini skirt or a

Chanel-type shift with long beads, white lipstick, and pilgrim shoes with big shiny buckles. Whoa, I felt a little like a weirdo at these parties. But Eddie Matos, who had a crush on me, always asked me to dance—salsa and rock. I guess I loved it when he said in a big Cuban accent, "I like *yourrr* style." When a group of us went to the RKO on Saturdays, he usually walked with me. But he hardly said anything. My real problem was not knowing whether to speak English or Spanish to him.

I definitely didn't get Latin boys. I didn't know how to be with them. Maybe I was smarter than they were. The funny thing was that with these guys, something told you not to show you were smarter. So, who was I supposed to be with them? Maritza, the innocent child of my Puerto Rey aunts, dead Cuban father, cocoon mother, murdered uncle and hidden cousins? Or an American girl at a private high school, who made the dean's list every term, listened to the Beatles and Stones, spoke perfect English without an accent, and who would have an important job one day? I know I'm sounding a little superior; I'm sure these guys had ideas for their future too, but they weren't the ones I had.

Then, those American boys from Power Memorial and Regis High Schools made virgin fruit punch (unless they spiked it) and played folk music, badly, but they were cool. Danny Finegan was the first American guy I had a real date with. Not at the neighborhood RKO or pizza place, but downtown at Radio City Music Hall to see "The Unsinkable Molly Brown" with Debbie Reynolds. We took the 8th Avenue train from Washington Heights where we lived, to the 59th street stop. I can't tell you how shocked I was when Mom told me it was the same train she took to the Roseland Ballroom when she was dating. Ugh! I thought everything I did was so unique!

Anyway, that night after burgers and black and white sundaes at Howard Johnson's, where we sat in turquoise and orange booths, Danny and I strolled back to the train station. He took my hand – his was a little clammy – and he swung our arms saying, "Ahh, just like strolling in Paris last summer."

There were little beads of sweat on Danny's upper lip, between the hairs of his almost-mustache. I tried not to giggle. Oh brother, what was he *gonna* do now, sing? Danny thought he was in a movie! He saw himself as very sophisticated since his student abroad trip in Europe last summer. He always kissed my cheek at the end of our dates. This was very cool, but I thought more was supposed to happen.

I was moving more and more to the side of becoming an American girl without even noticing. Everything I did just felt right to me. With my girls, I became a "411" telephone operator and an usher at the New York Coliseum for boat shows, car shows, the Shakespeare festival, and whatever else brought me out into the big world I was dying to live in. We practiced our flirting together with new groups of boys, and when things got a little dicey for one of us, we knew how to "go to the ladies' room for a moment" and scram.

To my Mom and the entire family, I was a total mystery who got A's in school, kept curfew and contributed part of any salary I made to the house. I was almost never home. I launched out to Long Island as a camp counselor for foster children and represented my Blessed Saints High School for Girls at summer summits in Washington, D.C. In a great act of finagling, I attended the Beatles' one and only concert in New York City. What did you wear to a Beatles' concert? Well, your shortest miniskirt and cutest poor-boy sweater, of course. Can you imagine, the Beatles? I was sitting in the audience of the Ed Sullivan Show, screaming with crazy love for those British boys.

I realized at this moment in time, that my mother was the tired queen of a very deflated cocoon, and I hadn't even graduated from high school yet! Then, at the beginning of my senior year, when I'm sixteen, I smashed a giant blow: Mother Superior called me into her office one morning and told me that she was going to award me a gift, sure to change the course of my life: a full academic scholarship to the St. Hilda's College for Women. This included board, though the college was only a train ride away in Westchester.

"*Not too far*," says Mother Bernadette in her brogue. "*So yar dear widow mother can see ya on weekends.*"

I was flabbergasted. What? I thought the nuns hated me. Four more years of obedience, living in the nun-cocoon? I'd be staying inside the perimeters of the way t*hey* saw the world—full of evil and danger around the corner. Sound familiar? I could barely make it out of the Mother Superior's office.

"Thank you, Mother," I say. "I'm undeserving."

"I knew there was humility inside ya, dear. Four years at St. Hilda's and the cheekiness in ya'll be polished right out. Yur such a smart girl fur yur kind."

As I turn to leave Mother's office on shaky knees, I scream NO inside every cell of my body even before I turn the brass knob.

My entire family was horrified by my will. They screamed, "You're on your own for college, then." And I was. I did it by getting myself into the best of the New York City University's colleges. Without blinking, as if propelled by an invisible engine, I made it happen with small yearly awards for grades, but mostly with after-school jobs. Making my way on a path that I entirely created for myself, was like a hot magic bullet propelling me into the future.

College was a brilliant place for me. My psychology-biology double major was supplemented with every literature, studio and art history course that I could possibly take. I went to parties at artist-professor studios. Don Noble was my sculpture teacher. He asked me to stay after everyone left, and my Catholic girl stepped in. I met Allen Ginsburg and Alexander Solzhenitsyn as a college host to visiting illuminati; and skirted around the actions of the SDS boys (Students for a Democratic Society) at Columbia, the details of which I best keep to myself.

But no one took my heart like the boy I met in a bar one night. In the long, dark saloon packed shoulder to shoulder with college kids, a good-looking boy in a tweed jacket and a lively mini-skirted girl caught each other's eyes from opposite ends of the room. That was me and the man I married later. Never mind party weekends at Yale with a current beau, or lab partners who wanted to become dates. I fell in love.

Our attraction was instant like sparks you saw in the night. We each had big dreams for our lives, spinning them in corner booths at late-night spots or parked at the Cloisters in a steamy Volkswagen bug. We had both suffered losses. We were hungry for each other in a way that grew without fear. He got me and couldn't believe that I was slowly becoming his. The boy was a sandy blond hunk—the way I liked. We became a perfect match, no matter the din of disapproval surrounding us.

Maritza
32
Then There's My Heart
New York City, 1960s–2000s

My heart quickened to its depths when I married the boy in the bar – and gave birth to two very special children. There was no turning back to aloneness ever again. That I could, with a loving but tumultuous man, walk my way into a life that I was creating by my own hand, was astounding. Trained under the trembling wings of my mother's fears, I threw her nonsense overboard and plunged ahead with great gusto. The boy and I were a dynamite duo, moving at lightning speed, and never ever doubting the value or goodness of our actions.

> Naked Chess
> They were still careening from the concert.
> Pounding from the bass
> Sliding on the vocals.
> At midnight they shimmied onto the board.
> Pawns caress the queen.
> White knight leaps over the bishop.
> Will rook surrender its treasure tonight?
> Doubtful

As trusty soldiers stand sentry over their charge.

From the boundary there is a movement.
It's the black knight advancing
Desire paving the way.
Pawns to king
Rook to bishop.
At one hour past midnight they are delivered.
Checkmate.
King and Queen
Disrobed on the board.
Naked chess.

Zooming on the relentless ambition of our professional careers generated currency of many kinds. "We deserve a ten-room apartment in an elegant landmark building. So what if we have to restore it—we're in the new, fancy Upper Westside." And we did just that. We had a decorator, nanny, and private schools for the children. It's how yuppies did it. "Let's buy that place in the country. Gotta get the kids out of the city." And, with a dreamy little tree house in Connecticut's Apple Hill, we lazed, swam, biked, played tennis, and discovered giant mushrooms in the woods. "The finances will sort themselves out: we'll just work harder!"

To be sure, I was the life-loving mother of my family, and finally, the complete child who lived in the midst of a real family: with a mother, a father, and children, children, children—mine and the gaggle of kids that were always at our house. My children skated in the foyer and scootered in the hall, turning the chic, new, white-pickled floors into the floorboards of a gym.

Given my superior training from a "super mother", mothering came easily and naturally to me. The children were my beauties. The boy was exactly who I imagined him to be: a handsome, vivacious elf with a giant loving heart. How did I ever, ever make this *niño rubio,* blond child? Yet his streak of comedy and wildness assured me he was one of my people. And my little girl. I knew her before she was. I dreamed of her before she was born—a wise little spirit who knew her own soul, a prescient beauty wearing dark curls and a white pinafore dress. Oh, the sweet visions of them that still remain: strands of hair the color of wheat in my boy's bowler cut; little toothmarks at the base of my girl's chubby, delicious thumb.

My children were magic. I became another girl with my girl Beth.

"Let's slide slowly on the ice, on Goose Pond, Mommy."

"Should we?"

"I'm scared."

"But there are ice fishermen in little shacks all over the pond. That means the ice is really, really thick, right?"

"What kind of a life is that for the poor fish?" Beth slid steadily forward in her moon boots. I was three steps ahead, just in case. When fog dropped down into the pond's afternoon, we were silent in the mist. We were together, sliding toward home.

My boy, Chris, was a noble, who fought the daggers of his education with pain and pluck. Wielding his *Skywalker* saber, he became an archeologist, a collector, and a lover of splashing battles that marked the events of history. When he was six, we visited the Fort of George Washington's battle on the Hudson, over, and over again. He finally asked if we could rent the Fort overnight, "So we can maybe hear the whispers of the soldiers fighting to make America."

But life was not all sweetness because the children were after all being raised by me, by us, who were full of warts and greedy dreams. There was the side of me who put everyone to bed, cleaned up, performed my duties as a wife and then started my graduate studies at midnight. I scribbled essays in a hot, steaming bathroom with a wheezing toddler on my lap. Finishing my doctorate and becoming a behavioral scientist was paramount. I was the one who skated, skated at high speed, round corners and bumps with a husband who was supportive—except when he was not. Our marriage was a long stretch of days, months, and years of closeness, distance, grand times, and closeness, distance, grand times, all over again. We were exhausted.

I was laser-clear within myself about my professional ambition. But I rarely admitted that openly because my other half would crumble to pieces. How ridiculous of me, as if he didn't notice? What I was really confused about was being a man's woman. No instructions for this, except to tolerate. There was bad behavior. The children mostly slept with *los angelitos* (the angels), except for later when things went bump in the night. A screaming man exploded down the hallway; a foot was slashed on broken glass; neighbors knocked at midnight. Harangues of "stupid boy," and "heartless woman," and our world almost came to an end.

Dark times. We rotated on a rumbling carousel of events as the children stared in silence. "Sepsis," doctors said. "It's the boy's entire body." Chris recovered. In my body, a tumor, the size of an orange was removed from my abdomen. When I came home, my little girl trembled at the sight of me.

"You look like a ghost, Mommy," she said. "How will you chase away the spiders in my dreams?"

Disease whittled away my husband's parents and they finally became the size they should have been. My beloved had no tears for them, he only made more bumps in the night. In one child's dream, someone pounded and pounded on the door during a storm. Our whole family shook and crouched in the hallway. The door finally crashed down— it was Daddy. But children do their best to grow, winding inner labyrinths that allow them to remember and forget, cope and withdraw

There was a ferociousness in me for so many years. I wanted so many things: a doctorate, expertise, publications, a tenured academic position and research grants. Not only did I follow this path, but I wildly careened down its edges. I was ambitious, driven, edgy and fat. During this time of my career adventures, I walked on shards of broken glass every day, never even missing a guru's balm on my feet. Sharpening my journey's edges were the eyes of senior colleagues, who saw me developing a cutting edge in my field. A *fascinoma,* maybe, a curious academic product of odd cultural determinants who was now standing shoulder to shoulder with them? The Puerto Reyan-Cuban woman (where is she from?) was a solid writer of creative theory even before she completed her post-doc training. There were commentaries, awards, and academic offerings. On the stage of professional conferences, I underlined the skewed politics of academic disciplines, whose assumptions about human behavior were steeped in the cultural value presuppositions of Western thought. My idea was to bring the essence of deep cultural dynamics *out* of the garlic-smelling, curry-cooking apartments of Astoria and Washington Heights, into the academic world's view.

Later, thinly veiling my heart, several research grants brought me overseas to investigate the travesty of a government lying to its people after exposing them to trauma, disease and incapacitation. Studying the survivors' fates both at home and in the broad diaspora, I saw families cope and fall, live and mourn. I was defending my own.

In today's parlance, I guess you would say that I tried to speak "truth to power," challenging current policy and paving a very teensy bit of the way into the depths of the tyrannized ethnic strangers, who were my family.

Maritza
33
Whole
Pacific Northwest, USA, 2024

I am a deep believer in the power of the past. The experiences that touch you as a child, shape your heart and hone your eye's lens for looking at the world. This is a miracle that happens deep inside your being that finally emerges as the person you become.

About my mother, I saw that she simply wanted to keep me, when my father died because I was her only love; when the Dictator crushed our family and she feared I would disappear; when I became an American girl, hungry for experiences far beyond her orbit. And finally, when I fell in love with an American man, a foreign creature, a stranger, and moved away from her. I would become twin pilots with this man, careening toward a twinkling galaxy of our own design. By standing staunch guard against my flight, Patti believed she could protect me from the losses that had crushed her own spirit long ago. But in the most honest parts of herself, Patti knew that I was her protection against loneliness. I was her only good thing. And I was leaving her.

My lift-off, therefore, wasn't easy. One evening, deciding that my intended and I were seeing too much of each other, Mom blocked my leaving the house with her own body. Sprawled on the floor directly across the front door, she moaned, "My heart. It's my heart."

"Mom, *Mami,* what is it?" I screamed. "I'm calling Dr. Freudenberg."

"Put that phone down," she screamed back.

"I'm getting our neighbor, Anna, then."

"Don't you dare, can't you see I'm in my house dress?"

I get what's going on. It's clear: my mother is blocking my life! With that thought, an energy ball begins to rumble in my chest that pushes out into my arms, giving me the strength of a Popeye who's just eaten a can of spinach. I undo the door's four locks, and with my new girl-super-strength, pull the door open as hard as I can, dragging my mother's limp, outstretched, whining body along with it. I simply step over her and leave, careful not to catch her house dress on my new patent leather heels.

The irony of this is that in the end, Mom's fear of losing me was in vain, because I loved and cared for her until her death, keeping her close by me. It was a complicated kind of love I had for her. It lived quietly inside me, leaking out only in moments of weakness, never reaching the levels of affectionate sparkle I offered as a child. I had to be extra careful, never risking needing her, no matter how lost I felt or scared of the prickling edges of my life. Divulge that I doubted my success? Tell her I argued with my husband? Confess that passivity was my greatest desire? Never. Because she would pull me inside her cocoon again, trapping me deep inside. I would never return from there again—it would be my death. I believed that.

But there was the rescue for my adult relationship with Mom: my children. She adored them, the new jewels of her existence, and with these little creatures who played inside her loving labyrinths, she was sated. In the earlier years, when she fought so hard against my loving others, she never considered that I might become exponential, bringing in and creating other beings to enter our lives and love us. These were my two children and my husband. My husband, she was fond of and respected his hard work as an attorney, but was never able to openly love him. The natural trope away from the giant who had literally stolen my heart—would always stop her.

I am older now and suppose that I have become more seasoned in the way my heart experiences the events of my life. This is certainly true of my father Gabriel's early death and being Patti's only child. As a very tiny girl, I hid in the closet, inside the comforting mustiness of shoes and clothes and sobbed for the frozen father in the picture with the baby in his arms. Later, after the one day of perfection with my uncle-father, Victor, I jammed the movie reel of memory on the frames of *Tío* and I walking across Central Park, me in my royal blue coat, he in his fedora hat. Was this a child's nostalgia, maybe even crocodile tears? Because I clearly was not destroyed by these losses.

So many, many nodal events have molded me. How did the murmurs of a sadistic dictatorship and the murder of my uncle sit with me over these years? A second father was lost to me when I was ten, as I barely stepped into the one day of experience of being a father's daughter. But strangely, after his death, I placed my Uncle Victor and the rest of my Puerto Rey family, in the deep unconscious spaces of my mind. Maybe, I needed to free my conscious self for growing.

It was around my early twenties, when I became a young mother, that a new rumbling of questions about my folks in Puerto Rey began to erupt. To my surprise, when I asked her, Mom did know about the fate of her brothers Milo and Dio; and she was willing to tell me. Speaking carefully, she said that Milo was lost only to his *Papá*. Milo had moved himself far, far away from the political ambitions of a father who saw him as merely an extension of himself. But Milo, she said, had in fact moved toward something big: family love and the warmth of nurturance that he had lost upon his mother's death. Married to his first love, Fernanda, Milo proudly raised ten children and remained the official schoolmaster and an unofficial attorney in his town, until his death.

"It is Dio who truly became lost to the family and himself," said Mom sadly. "What I know about his last days is that only a few months before Victor's own killing, Dio appeared out of nowhere at his house, emaciated and probably dying. It was a terrible time then, under the Galante regime, when countless people were running and hiding to evade arrest for who knows what infraction against that terror government. Victor cleaned and fed Dio, hid him in the garden shed overnight, and demanded absolute secrecy from his family about the visit. The next morning Dio was gone, never to be seen again. Poor Victor took his brother's fate to his own grave." Mom was in tears when she finished the story, and I knew that pressing her further about other members of the family would be impossible.

It was, of course, my reliable Aunt Rose, Rosina Dorada, who told me about my Uncle Victor's family, after the murder. From my images of childhood, I thought of the family on the veranda of my dreams—where were they now? Who were they now? I had lost track of them. I was so in love with them once. They were Aunt Julia, Uncle Victor's wife, and their four children, my cousin-siblings, *primos-hermanos* as they say in the Caribbean, because that's how close your blood is. What finally became of them after the shooting?

When Uncle Victor was murdered in Puerto Rey, Aunt Julia and the two wounded older boys, Victor Jr. and Ronny, were taken to different hospitals. Further attempts were made on their lives there with overdoses of medicine, even with guards placed at their doors. The two youngest children, Anita and Harry, were finally found in a police interrogation center, soiled, hungry, and dazed. The story goes that Anita, six, wailed over the blood that splattered her legs and white sox. Her Daddy's blood. "I'm sorry,

Mami, I'm sorry I got my sox dirty." She had no memory of the massacre.

The government of a European country provided the family asylum and protection, honoring a commitment they had made to Victor just before his death. After burying Victor on their last day in Catalina, my always-reserved Aunt Julia, made a broadcast statement that also appeared in several international papers. She let the public know that Puerto Rey had become a place where people could not speak, think, or really live a full life anymore. "Brutality," she said, "is all around us." The country of asylum generously housed and protected Uncle Victor's family for years. They were placed deep in the country's interior, in a recently constructed town whose walls still smelled of wet concrete.

I found my aunt and cousins many years later on the West Coast of the US, where they had ultimately migrated after the asylum years in Europe and after the final fall of Puerto Rey's Galante dictatorship in 1965. The cousins are adults like me, now, already moving along the tracks of their tumultuous pasts and individual destinies. Victor Jr., the restless and temperamental oldest son, was a real estate developer who had made lots of money and lost lots of money, living the life of a playboy, between marriages.

"Maritza," he told me over some beers. "Do you know what it's like to see your father's face blown away? I was sixteen. I took a bullet for him and he still died. I've been troubled all my life."

Harry, Uncle Victor and Aunt Julia's handsome youngest son was deceased. Restless during the asylum years after his father's killing, Harry didn't timidly hover around Julia like the others. He joined the town's boy gangs and terrified his siblings with meanness. Macho was his code word. When the family finally moved to the U.S., Harry's erratic behavior continued until his premature death in a racing derby. Against his family's pleas, Harry drove an uncertified car and crashed on the track.

I found Ronny, the middle son, to be as solid and even-tempered as his brothers were not. Father of five children and husband to a magnificent American woman, Ronny, is the family's safe haven. This many-times decorated police homicide detective says in his stolid style, "Well, somebody's *gotta* get the bad guys." Ronny shapes his life by vanquishing the death of his father over, and over again.

And finally, there is Anita, the only girl, and the cousin I am mystified by. The horrors of the Galante dictatorship years etched a clear and deep path for her life. This professor of Latin American history begins her real job at night, after days in the classroom. Unencumbered by personal relationships or the fusses of everyday life, Anita has taken upon herself, the research and accounting of every kidnapping, torture, disappearance, and murder perpetrated by the decades-long Galante government in Puerto Rey. The work is voluminous, and the detail is staggering. Oh, how close to her own father's actions she is—secretly disseminating records of state-sanctioned violence, just like her dad did. The printing press in the sub-basement has simply moved upstairs to the global internet.

Anita is surely her father's daughter, but isn't every one of us a composite of our early internalizations? Those whose bosoms cradled us and whose hands tended us are now integral parts of our psychologies. Either we become them or formulate complex ways of becoming their foil—not them. Some solutions to these dynamics are reasonable and adaptive; other solutions burn our lives. Some of us may hear the enraged voice of our irrational mother as we scold our own children. Others may crumble like a father who sabotaged his personal success. I was determined to never fear the world, a position so counter to my mother's. Oh, these kin! While we fight to remain unconscious of their presence, we do what they did—or not; feel what they felt—or avoid feeling; and hold a world view that is as if we are looking through their eyes. Oh yes, yes, of course, we also become our autonomous selves, with strength and resilience and freshly developed modes of coping with the world. But let's not fool ourselves; our kin live vibrantly inside us.

In high school, as I was growing in leaps and bounds, I harbored the secret fear that, apart from how much I loved my aunt, Nina, I would grow mad and paranoid like her. The notion wasn't far-fetched, given the admonitions of my family who believed that one cause of Nina's mental illness was her compulsive book reading. So, to ensure against my aunt's possible madness in me, I became a behavioral scientist. And to put extra icing on that cake, I completed a doctorate, investigating how schizophrenia manifested in different parts of the world! It was, no doubt, my love for Nina, that drove me to understand the workings of her particular kind of mind.

How my family has propelled me. What would I have done without the fire of my Aunt Rose, Rosina Dorada—the possessor of brilliance and guts and a good amount of "get out of my way?" I've needed Rosina's passion over the years, as the influence of my mother's fears and reticence have plagued me more than I like to admit. Patti and Rose are, without a doubt, the dual mothers who inhabit the depths of my psyche. But I've learned something new in the writing of this story, thanks to the sensibilities of a close and loving friend: my insistent characterization of *Mami's* fearfulness belies the strongest part of her—her absolute fierceness in protecting me. She was the staunch defender who staved off the dangers of the external world for me (real or imagined!) until I could finally become whole.

I've learned about Rose too: my hero-woman, my empress aunt. She knew every family secret. While her generous heart rescued so many of us, I've come to understand now that Rose was also a complex and imperfect woman. She gave life and love in large sweeping gestures: mothering her mother's children; initiating the American lives of her sisters; nursing the disturbed Nina until the end of both their days. And, when business success and ownership gave her the means, Rose's giving arms went outside the family, supporting the efforts of many people who simply wanted to come to America to educate themselves and lead open lives.

In the early 1960s, when Galante went beyond the pale killing and kidnapping thousands of Puerto Reyans, Rose and her Jorge extended extraordinary gestures. Raising thousands for the explicit project of toppling the tyrant, they were part of a Puerto Reyan underground in the US. But their grandest gesture came in the form of two adolescent girls, brother Milo's only daughters, who they brought to the U.S. and raised, lest they also be taken and exploited by the dictator's men.

The human capacity to love and emotionally attend to the needs of others, however, is a multifaceted ability. Large, loving, generous gestures do not necessarily parallel the ability to also read another's personal fear or terror of being alone. I must admit that as much as I adored my aunt, I also recognized this was a fault in her. Nowhere was this more obvious than in her inability to understand the feelings of the two young girls she brought to America - Milo's girls. They are now the strong adult women of their own American households. However, this is many years after I heard their sobs and saw their loneliness, as Rose dutifully educated them, made them American citizens and refined their English; but never understood their wrenching from loving parents, their bedwetting, or their early fears of attending an American school. For Rose, the big picture was what counted: a secure American environment and an education. Love takes many forms.

Finally, I must tell you the last story about my complex Aunt Rose. I don't like it because it makes her idealized glow fade a little more for me. Rose had a son. His name was Horacio, and he was the child of Manuel Goya. Remember Rose confiding in Patti about her last sexual encounter with Goya resulting in a pregnancy?

The child's birth was a secret everyone knew. Rose barely spoke of the baby boy, who she could not bring herself to integrate into her new American life. How ironic and repetitive family life can sometimes be. Rose hired Miss Eva at the very familiar Colegio Metodista in Puerto Rey to be his caretaker while she lived in New York. So like baby Victor such a long time ago...

"When he's two years old, I'll bring him to the U.S... when he's five," said Rose. She finally brought him at age eight and then placed him in a boarding school in Montreal, Canada.

Horacio was the best-dressed boy at school who was coveted for his many toy airplanes. But alas, he lived with his mother Rose only on holidays, during the days he was not with Goya in Puerto Rey. Is it a wonder the boy became a professional pilot, forever searching for the arrival of his mother from the sky?

The writing of this story has left me with a great surprise. I have always wondered who I would be now if my father had remained in my life. I will never know. All I have is the little bit of Gabriel I got. But I finally realize that I have sculpted the image of fatherliness from the collective hearts of all the men who have been part of my life. My father is my grandfather, General Bernardo, the paternal dictator, the *Papá* who tried to care for his family like little soldiers, as he galloped off to shape the horizons of his country, his patria. My father is my sweetie, Uncle Jorge, Rose's husband, the real partner of her life, and the one I tried so hard to make believe belonged to me. My father is my Uncle Victor, our family's hero with the courage to know he would be taken away from those he loved.

"Sometimes," he said. "A bigger voice pushes you to care for something more than the everyday of your life: your country, your people and the ones who are suffering."

My life is filled now with the family I created for myself: my husband, my two children, and our four grandchildren. But every day, I think of the six brave children who surrounded my grandmother, Estrella, on her deathbed. They are, in fact, all around me. I live in the foothills of the Cascade Mountains now, where evergreens and red cedars tower above the surface of these great magnum stones. I see trees swaying at the top ridge. It's my family in the sunshine. They're waving to me and dancing! It's my mother Patti and my aunts Rose and Nina, and my uncles Victor, Dio, Milo and Jorge. My grandparents, General Bernardo and Estrella are swaying softly in the breeze. My father Gabriel is there, and he is dancing for me too.

THE END

References

Hanson, E. (2014). Fly. *Voyage.* Troutdale: thepoeticunderground.